INFINITELY

Woodbrooke College

SARUM THEOLOGICAL LECTURES

INFINITELY BELOVED

The Challenge of Divine Intimacy

Brian Thorne

DARTON · LONGMAN + TODD

First published in 2003 by
Darton, Longman and Todd Ltd
1 Spencer Court
140–142 Wandsworth High Street
London sw18 4JJ

ISBN 0–232–52507–2

A catalogue record for this book is available from the British Library.

Designed by Sandie Boccacci
Phototypeset in 11¼/14pt Bembo by Intype Libra Ltd
Printed and bound in Great Britain
by The Bath Press, Bath

For Debbie,
who has the courage to accept her belovedness

CONTENTS

Acknowledgements   ix

Prologue: A RELUCTANT PROPHET   I

1 JOURNEYS IN RELATIONSHIP:
   JULIAN OF NORWICH AND CARL ROGERS   7

2 A COMMUNITY OF HEALING:
   GEORGE LYWARD AND FINCHDEN MANOR   22

3 THE SURVEILLANCE CULTURE
   AND ECONOMIC IMPERIALISM   37

4 THE REDEMPTION OF SEXUALITY
   AND THE EVOLUTION OF HUMANITY   53

5 LETTING GO AND LETTING BE:
   THE PROCESS OF DIVINISATION   68

Epilogue: A CLARION CALL TO THE CHURCH   86

Notes   88
List of References   92

ACKNOWLEDGEMENTS

This book is a slightly amended version of the Sarum Theological Lectures given in April/May 2002. I have added a Prologue and an Epilogue in order to provide a context and in some way to explain to myself, as well as to my readers, why I decided to accept what at first sight seemed such an unlikely invitation. To travel from Norwich to Salisbury on five consecutive Thursdays is no mean undertaking and to deliver lectures in the somewhat awesome setting of Salisbury Cathedral no task for the faint-hearted. Suffice it to say that, in retrospect, I have no regrets. Through the acceptance of the invitation I learned much about myself and found the courage to face aspects of my own experiencing which I had previously been reluctant to acknowledge. If in the process I have managed to cast some light on what it means to be made in the image and likeness of God and to share the life of the Holy Trinity, then I shall be more than content. It is my growing conviction that without such developing awareness there is little hope that as a species we can survive. Much that has happened since I gave the lectures has only served to reinforce that conviction.

My reception in Salisbury on each occasion was generous in the extreme and I am deeply appreciative of the committed audience who stayed with me throughout the series. More particularly, I am indebted to David Catchpole and his colleagues at Sarum College who provided such convivial hospitality and to the Dean and Chapter of Salisbury Cathedral for the use of one of the finest buildings in Christendom. To Philip and Susie Sheldrake I owe perhaps the greatest debt for it was they who had the confidence in me to put forward my name as a prospective lecturer in the first place. My one sadness is that Susan

Howatch, whose generosity made the lectures possible, was unable to be present. Her example in finding new ways of communicating the ways of God to an unchurched generation is an abiding inspiration.

As always, my warmest thanks go to my wife for tolerating yet more absences and to my long-suffering colleagues at the University of East Anglia and the Norwich Centre for humouring me in what must sometimes seem the musings of a mystical maverick. Finally, my thanks to Megan Craven at the Norwich Centre for her meticulous word-processing and to Virginia Hearn at Darton, Longman and Todd for her attentiveness and generosity of spirit in seeing this venture through.

BRIAN THORNE
October 2002

A RELUCTANT PROPHET

My first reaction on being invited to give the 2002 Sarum Lectures was one of incredulity. I am not a theologian, nor a philosopher or sociologist of religion. It seemed unlikely that my undoubted love of cathedrals was sufficient reason for the luminaries of Sarum College to invite me to speak on five separate occasions in the awesome setting of Salisbury Cathedral. Attempts to persuade me that my work as a person-centred therapist,[1] allied to my Christian commitment, gave me a special perspective on the 'psychological–theological interface' left me only partially convinced. In the end, I was forced to search within myself for the essential motivation and rationale for repeatedly undertaking the tiresome journey from Norwich to Salisbury – a weekly pilgrimage which revealed the stress and tension involved in travelling by public transport in twenty-first-century Britain. My recurrent nightmare (fortunately not fulfilled) was of entering Salisbury Cathedral just in time to see an angrily departing audience who had given up waiting in vain for my arrival on yet another delayed train.

It was only gradually that I realised the full significance of the opportunity which I was being offered and that all I had to do was to consider myself worthy of the invitation and to accept it. Once this hurdle had been surmounted, I could realistically appraise the resources that I possessed and settle to the task. For a person-centred therapist, the discipline of his or her profession requires a repeated engagement with what, in our jargon, is called the 'flow of experience within'. What, I asked myself, were the most intense or persistent feelings and thoughts which preoccupied me, for it was they which would reveal the essential resources for my task? The disconcerting outcome of the exercise of this therapeutic discipline was the discovery that I was subject to two apparently conflicting and alternating states of being – passionate hope and passionate anger. The latter state was not easy for me to acknowledge, let alone to own, for it was a considerable threat to my self-concept. I like to think of myself as a patient, compassionate man who is committed to his therapeutic and teaching work and to the pursuit of peace, harmony and reconciliation. I am often told, and sometimes believe, that my most lasting contribution to the literature of person-centred therapy will prove to be a piece I wrote nearly twenty years ago entitled *The Quality of Tenderness* (Thorne, 1985). Certainly I see myself as someone who seeks to engage in depth with those who suffer and who knows the power of tenderness in the healing of wounds, from which to varying degrees we all suffer. This tenderness finds a ready partner in hope for the two qualities powerfully combine to offer a psychological and emotional climate in which pain can be faced and transcended. But if I knew myself to be an essentially hopeful person, it was the discovery of the passionate and persistent anger which at first alarmed me and then revealed the even more unnerving possibility that I was going to Salisbury as a prophet. What is more, if hope was to be the prophet's inspiration, anger, it seemed, was to be his driving force.

Perhaps prophets have always been both hopeful and angry people. After all, to engage in prophetic warnings scarcely makes sense unless the prophet is fired by a concern for the future and hopes – perhaps against all hope – that everything can somehow turn out well or, at the very least, that catastrophe can be averted. The prophet who has no hope for the future is little more than a doom-monger who spreads despair and despondency among his contemporaries. Not infrequently, however, it is anger which provides the energy to persevere when the prophet is rebuffed or when the message seems to fall on deaf ears. The prophetic task is often a thankless one and the anger which springs from passionate concern ensures that the prophet does not succumb to the first signs of determined opposition from those who have much invested in their own agendas.

It is easy enough to be angry with those who are overtly destructive or manifestly self-seeking. Their behaviour is usually only too blatant and anger is an appropriate and often socially sanctioned response. It is much more difficult to access anger when it is engendered by rational and responsible men and women who are seemingly committed to the common good. It may indeed be that my difficulty in owning my anger springs not only from my reluctance to put at risk my self-concept as a compassionate, caring person but also from my unwillingness to believe that well-intentioned, thoughtful people can, in fact, embody lethal attitudes which, inevitably, result in highly destructive outcomes. What is even more sinister is the level of corporate unawareness which makes such attitudes and behaviour not only endemic but socially and politically acceptable.

As a therapist, much of my work involves the forming of relationships where suffering human beings can feel safe enough to face their pain and, in so doing, increase their awareness of themselves and of others. It is precisely such relating and such awareness which then enable a person to move through life with enhanced self-confidence and sense of self-worth. Invariably, too, I discover that, given a relationship where they feel genuinely accepted and understood, almost all those who seek my help begin to reveal the wonder of their own natures. They become more self-acceptant and, as a result, more responsive to others. They are also better able to harness their various gifts and abilities in the service of the wider community. It is the therapist's privilege to glimpse daily the potential in the human being for self-transcendence and this even in those cases where the starting point has been the anguish of abuse or the experience of lifelong abandonment and neglect. Such transformation is not the result,

I believe, of the therapist's superior psychological knowledge or even of his or her therapeutic skill. What matters is his or her ability to enter into relational depth where the person seeking help feels profoundly accepted, and where the therapist is perceived as someone who genuinely wishes to understand and who does not hide behind a mask of pseudo-professionalism.

My passionate trust in the essential wonder of human nature and in the creative potential of humankind is undoubtedly affirmed and enhanced by my daily experience as a therapist. To be a frequent witness to minor miracles is assuredly a powerful recipe for the maintenance of hope. At the end of a day, I am often astonished to reflect on the extraordinary glimpses I have caught of human beings fully alive and I know that such aliveness (which St Irenaeus once described as the glory of God) has resulted from the liberation of spirit engendered by the deeply empathic acceptance which, at its best, person-centred therapy offers to even the most self-rejecting and distressed individuals. For them, empathy and acceptance are the royal road to self-affirmation and a life worth living.

In the face of such incontrovertible evidence of human resilience and potential, it is perhaps scarcely surprising that much that characterises our current culture induces in me an increasing sense of outrage. In the therapy room, I seek to offer myself to others without pretence and to extend to them an acceptance and an empathic understanding which is restorative and points to life and hope. In society at large, however, it is the absence of precisely these same qualities which permeates the very fabric of our collective experience. Judgementalism, litigious aggression, cut-throat competitiveness, fear of failure are the hallmarks of a society which rides roughshod over the needs and aspirations of human beings made in the image of God and gives the primacy instead to the achievement of economic superiority and the maintenance of what is ironically called a high standard of living. Oil, it would seem, is more important than the spilling of human blood, the possession of a third motor car more important than the relief of starvation or the preservation of the planet's fragile ecology. Those who argue that in the Western world we have in the last three hundred years progressively suppressed our intuitive, empathic and spiritual mode of consciousness and given unquestioning supremacy to the rational, analytical and scientific mode are, I believe, groping towards an important aspect of the process which has landed us in a situation where the very future of the planet and of the human species hangs in the balance.

My anger, then, is with the seeming indifference of those politicians, educationists, captains of industry, church leaders and innumerable others who, when the obvious is staring them in the face, refuse to acknowledge that human beings are fast losing their *élan vital* as the planet rushes towards disaster. I find it almost beyond comprehension that intelligent men and women who clearly wish to lead decent lives and do care about the future can nonetheless cultivate the studied unawareness which perpetuates and even reinforces attitudes which are death dealing. Perhaps nothing illustrates this more grotesquely than the current pursuit of the so-called war on terrorism.[2] Instead of seizing the opportunity for honest self-exploration and the kind of dialogue which only an empathic intent can possibly render productive, it would seem that the leaders of the developed world, together with the majority of their fellow citizens, seek refuge in demonising the aggressor and protecting their own way of life. This is not to defend the barbarous acts of terrorism which have been perpetrated in recent times. It is simply to question whether the age-old response to such acts is any longer a viable option. The attitudes of judgement, condemnation, dehumanisation and retaliation which have as their final objective the destruction of the wicked aggressor are no longer defensible without running the risk of global warfare and the annihilation of the human species. Sadly, however, because such attitudes are embedded in the very fabric of our culture and permeate our daily lives there seems little chance of escaping the vicious circle. Only a revisioning of who we are and a recognition that, as a species, we are beloved from the beginning of time can possibly bring about the evolution of consciousness that will be necessary if we are to celebrate our membership one of another and love as God loves.

As I stood in Salisbury Cathedral and delivered the original text of the five chapters which follow I was intermittently aware that my words were outrageous. Even now I do not know if they were the utterances of a reluctant prophet buoyed up by hope and energised by anger or the outpourings of a naïve and self-inflated babbler. What I do know, however, is that if the Holy Spirit is anywhere to be found in what follows, the Christian era, far from drawing to a close, is only now about to begin.

JOURNEYS IN RELATIONSHIP: JULIAN OF NORWICH AND CARL ROGERS

Thirty-five years' experience as a person-centred therapist convinces me that for many of us the desire for intimacy rules our lives while our actual experience of relationships often brings about a profound fear of the very thing that we most desire. We are not, it would seem, made for solitude and yet the pain of betrayal, misunderstanding, rejection, abuse or abandonment can be so devastating that the prospect of closeness becomes terrifying because it carries with it the dread of yet more suffering. So fundamental are the desire for intimacy and at the same time the horror of it proving treacherous that not only individuals but whole communities founder on the rock of alienation which can so easily turn to despair and destructiveness. My own view, contrary to that of some others, is that the rapid development in recent years of electronic communication and information technology has done nothing to alleviate this alienation.[1] On the contrary, by offering the semblance of dialogue and interconnectedness, the new technology has served to reveal the barrenness of the interpersonal world which many of us inhabit much of the time. As I am obliged to listen to the vacuous conversations on mobile 'phones which so often fill the carriages of railway trains these days, I grow sad at the apparent sterility of many of the relationships which they reveal. I am angry, too, that this empty chatter often implies an indifference to those who are physically present and little respect for their well-being. Equally disturbing is the sight of many individuals glued to their mobile 'phones as they walk down the street oblivious, it would seem, of other passers-by and blind to the environment through which they are passing. When motorists are guilty of similar behaviour it becomes all too obvious that they are endangering the lives of others. It is perhaps less obvious that the growing addiction to communicating on the hoof with absent persons while in the close proximity of those who are present in the flesh is a form of assault and helps to intensify the coldness of a culture where persons are continually reified by the behaviour of others.

Reification is a pompous word to denote the process by which a person is deprived of his or her essential personhood by being rendered a commodity or an object to be used or exploited. A reified person no longer has to be related to. He or she can be treated as an 'it' or ignored altogether. This loss of personhood can engender rage in the victim but more likely it will induce a low-level depression which permeates the fabric of an individual's being. As a therapist I know that behind much inarticulate despair or unexpressed rage there lingers still the almost extinguished yearning for intimacy. There remains the forlorn hope that to experience such intimacy could mean restoration to personhood but restoration seems so improbable and the risk of further reification so great that the yearning is often swallowed up in fear and cynicism. My decision to embark upon this series of reflections springs nonetheless from my conviction that it is indeed through intimacy that we have the chance to be persons rather than individuals. Sadly, however, through my work as a therapist I am daily caught up in a culture where the experience of intimacy seems rare. It is difficult to avoid the appalling thought that persons as opposed to individuals are now an endangered species. If this gloomy analysis is only half correct then the responsibility of offering what little I know of the redemptive possibilities of human intimacy becomes all the more imperative. More important still, I cannot keep to myself the discovery that at the heart of the cosmos there is an energy which calls me into intimate relationship with itself and through that very calling reveals that it is no 'it' but contains within itself the essence of personhood. If as I attempt the proclamation of this 'good news' I find myself squirming with embarrassment in my academic and professional skin, then this, regretfully, will have to be the cost. At least, I shall have the satisfaction of knowing that I have not been a coward even if I have risked revealing myself as a fool and perhaps an arrogant one at that.

Friday mornings have particular significance for me and it is there that I wish to begin. The day usually starts with my attendance at the Shrine of Julian of Norwich for the early morning Eucharist. My fourteenth-century fellow citizen is an inexhaustible source of encouragement and inspiration.[2] It still gives me a thrill to remember that over 600 years ago Julian was counselling from her anchoress's cell at the side of St Julian's church in medieval King Street. For me, the cell – rebuilt after the Second World War – is hallowed ground. Not only is it nowadays part of the church itself but on a Friday morning, when the prayers of the pilgrims who have visited during the week are offered up, Julian herself seems palpably present offering her deep insight into the nature of God and of humanity. In her company I know that all is well and all shall be well even on those occasions when my life is stressful in the extreme and I am beset by seemingly intractable difficulties.

Julian's pervasive power stems from her absolute conviction, thanks to the visions she received on 8 May 1373, that God does not accuse us because it is not in his nature to do so. On the contrary, Julian tell us that he regards us with the utmost tenderness and longs for us to respond to his love, which is beyond our wildest dreams. In her visions Julian sees no anger in God: she sees only a love which in the Passion and Crucifixion finds its expression in the willingness to suffer to the uttermost. So great is that love, that Jesus tells Julian that if he could he would have suffered more. The suffering man on the cross suddenly breaks into a radiant smile – love for the beloved is so intense that the privilege of suffering the agony of crucifixion and dereliction brings in its wake an indescribable joy. This is not the sacrificial victim burdened and weighed down by the sins of the world. It is the passionate lover who embraces suffering and death because love finds in such self-giving its perfect expression. Julian is overwhelmed; she listens with astonishment as her good Lord tells her: 'It is a joy, a bliss, an endless delight to me that ever I suffered my Passion for you; and if I could suffer more, I should suffer more.' (Colledge and Walsh, 1978: 216). In incredulous amazement she realises that such love constitutes the incontrovertible evidence of how much we are esteemed and honoured by the God who made us: 'We are his bliss, we are his reward, we are his honour, we are his crown. And this was a singular wonder and a most delectable contemplation, that we are his crown.' (Colledge and Walsh, 1978: 216). And still Julian could not really bring herself to believe what her experience told her was true. Her mind strives to understand and to accept what she knows in her inmost being.

> What I am describing now is so great joy to Jesus that he counts as nothing his labour and his sufferings and his cruel and shameful death. And in these words: If I could suffer more, I should suffer more, I saw truly that as often as he could die, so often should he die, and love would never let him rest till he had done it. And I contemplated with great diligence to know how often he should die if he would. And truly the number so far exceeded my understanding and intelligence that my reason had not leave or power to comprehend or accept it. (Colledge and Walsh, 1978: 217)

As I sit in the Shrine early on a Friday morning, my mind is stilled, my anxiety soothed. The truth which Julian received in 1373 communicates itself to my twenty-first-century soul and finds there a ready reception. Every Friday morning I am reconfirmed in the personal knowledge, which, through no merit of my own, first entered my being on a Good Friday afternoon in 1946 when I was a boy of nine.

I find it difficult still to claim a kinship with my illustrious fellow citizen for I know only too well the calumny to which she has been subjected and the ridicule in which her revelations are often held. Not long ago I was sent an essay – not by the writer but by a female third party so that I could have a 'right of reply' – attacking my own work and accusing me of falling apart intellectually whenever I moved from psychotherapeutic discourse into irrational nonsense about Christ and the Church. I had not asked for this essay and could not know whether the person who sent it to me (whom I had met only once) was seeking to undermine me or to find comfort for herself. What rapidly became apparent, however, was that the essayist was no friend of Julian. On the contrary, he roundly condemned her as a person riddled with superstition and possessed of a barbaric imagination which revelled in the blood and gore of the crucifixion. In the face of such hostility, I became frighteningly conscious of my own vulnerability especially when I consider that my own 'revelation' in a war-torn Bristol park also involved an encounter with the suffering Christ on the cross[3] (Thorne, 1991a). For me, however, as for Julian, the knowledge which penetrated my young soul as a result of that encounter had nothing to do with a sense of guilt or sinfulness. It was rather a conviction of being loved beyond my wildest imagination and of having within me the capacity for responding to that love with an equally passionate intensity. What is more there came at the time and intermittently ever since the realisation that in the light of my infinite belovedness and my infinite capacity to love, nothing else matters in the least. Again, as I recall that my boyhood experience was given me in 1946 not long after the end of a bitter World War and that Julian, too, lived in a time of appalling conflict, plague and disaster, the bond between us strengthens. The difference, of course, is that she lived in a time of faith whereas I have lived through a period of increasing secularisation and have come to see Christianity, to quote Cardinal Murphy-O'Connor, Archbishop of Westminster, as 'all but vanquished' and the Church marginalised — the subject of scornful indifference or worse for many in our contemporary society.

I suppose that for me the Friday morning Eucharist in Julian's Shrine is a kind of lovers' tryst. In Julian's presence I am free to acknowledge my own nature without the complication of being thought mad or arrogant. Supported by her understanding I am able to let myself relax in the presence of a God who shares my humanity so that I may confidently share his divinity. This overwhelming conviction of participating in the loving activity of the Holy Trinity extends to all those who are present. As we share the peace, this motley collection of somewhat sleepy worshippers experiences a transformation. For an instant we know that 'all is well' because we dare to claim our rightful place as lovers and beloved in the eternal dance. Julian must delight to be with us for she knew our experience in her earthly sojourn and wrote it down:

> God the blessed Trinity, who is everlasting being, just as he is eternal in that beginning, just so was it in his eternal purpose to create human nature, which fair nature was first prepared for his own Son, the second person; and when he wished by full agreement of the whole Trinity he created us all at once. And in our creation he joined and united us to himself, and through this union we are kept as pure and as noble as we were created. (Colledge and Walsh, 1978: 293)

I emerge from St Julian's Church and walk into the city with a friend of more than twenty years. She has been a spiritual companion who, through her struggles with mental illness, has harrowed hell and taken heaven by storm. The city is always friendly even if it is raining, which seems seldom to be the case.

I am astonished how often rain ceases and clouds clear just at this moment when the little band of love-intoxicated worshippers emerges from the church, including Luke, Sister Pamela's piously mischievous dog, who then greets Di's three dogs who have been patiently waiting in the car for their mistress to arrive from her devotions. The animal world's intermingling with our own is reflected in the streets of Norwich at this early hour. Dogs and cats are sniffing the air and the buildings, too, seem to be preparing for the day. This interconnectedness of all things is somehow orchestrated by the plethora of medieval churches which still abound in central Norwich. St John's Timberhill, St Stephen's, St Peter Mancroft all come into view as we walk and the spire of the magnificent cathedral of the Holy and Undivided Trinity is always visible. Just out of sight are St Giles on the Hill, St George's Tombland and St John, Maddermarket. These astonishing buildings speak of an age when despite war and pestilence and unspeakable suffering, the world for most people made some kind of sense. Their churches spoke of an invisible reality which informed their inner life and gave a sense of journeying onwards. Long before Charles Darwin there was, I believe, a sense of evolution, of movement towards a greater fullness of being which transcended death and could lead to the heavenly courts of eternal bliss.

Later on a Friday morning, I am reminded of the experience of the interconnectedness of all things and of the evolutionary journey as I sit with clients in the calm environment of the Norwich Centre Counselling Service. My work as a counsellor and psychotherapist – for many years exercised primarily within the context of a university – now takes place in a fine Victorian house situated opposite the Roman Catholic cathedral and next door to the Jewish synagogue. The Centre, established in 1979, was the first counselling agency in Europe to be committed to the person-centred approach to therapy originated by the American psychologist Dr Carl Rogers and his associates. Dr Rogers died in 1987 at the age of 85 but he came to Norwich in 1984 and, with solemn purposefulness, sat in every room in the Norwich Centre as if to test out the quality of the therapeutic environment. He pronounced the 'vibrations' to be good and subsequently sent us a fine photograph of himself which still hangs on the wall of our reception office. In the same way that Julian often seems very present in her Shrine so, too, does Carl Rogers in the rooms and corridors of the Norwich Centre. A small statue of Julian resides on a corner shelf just outside the office and it amuses me to imagine that she and Carl sometimes meet up to 'mardle' in Norfolk style in the 'right merry' atmosphere of the heaven that Julian in her earthly life was privileged to glimpse.

Carl Rogers is not always greatly esteemed these days within the groves of academe or in the cut-throat world of professional psychology. His view of human nature is frequently regarded as overly optimistic and even naïve, while his approach to psychotherapy is seen as lacking professional rigour and making unrealistic and dangerously risky demands on the therapist. In church and theological circles the response to Rogers is often equally ambivalent or hostile. The fact that he trained for Christian ministry but abandoned his theological formation for a career in psychology hardly promises him an enthusiastic reception in the ecclesiastical world. He is often accused of ignoring the reality of Original Sin and of encouraging an individualistic 'selfism' which is in fundamental opposition to the Christian ethic of selfless service (cf. Vitz, 1977). Rogers, it would seem, inhabits a lonely position with no enduring esteem in the ranks of either the psychologists or the theologians. Interestingly, however, he continues to be regarded, even by psychologists, as one of the most influential figures in twentieth-century psychology and psychotherapy and his books are still to be found in most major bookshops. For me it is a cause for considerable satisfaction that my retirement is cushioned thanks to the royalties from the annual reprinting of my study of his life and work (Thorne, 1992) and by the fact that the book which I co-authored with my atheist colleague, Professor Dave Mearns of Strathclyde University, on Rogers' approach to therapy has sold more copies than any book in any discipline published by the prestigious academic publishers Sage of London (Mearns and Thorne, 1999). What is more, as I listen to the constant ringing of the 'phone and the buzz of the doorbell at the Norwich Centre I need no further proof that this great but humble American frontiersman has contributed a powerful gift to humanity.

The first client is Charlotte. I do not need to describe the nature of her problem or anything of her life history although it happens to be traumatic and punctuated by the episodes of appalling violence and abuse with which I am sadly all too familiar. Often, I marvel that many of my clients are alive at all let alone that they still have the courage to battle with their suffering and to make sense of their lives. What matters to me, however, as it mattered supremely to Carl Rogers, is that Charlotte is a human being, a person.

Rogers, as I have said, had originally intended to be a Christian minister but part way through his training at Union Theological Seminary he literally crossed the street to Teachers' College to begin the study of psychology. He had decided that he could not in all conscience commit himself to a life where he would be required not only to believe a series of dogmatic statements of faith but also to preach them to others. Such a commitment was at variance with his growing conviction that, in the last analysis, only his own experience with its multiplicity of thoughts, feelings and perceptions could be a tolerably reliable guide to belief and action. Institutional religion – even of the liberal and progressive kind which he found at Union – was likely, he came to believe, to act as an impediment to discovering his own truth. In all probability his decision to part company with the Church and, as it turned out, with Christianity was further influenced by his boyhood and adolescent experiences of what he called the benevolent despotism of his parents who were deeply committed to a fundamentalist version of evangelical Christianity. The conditionality of his parents' acceptance was increasingly resented by Rogers and until the end of his life, while never doubting their good intentions and the sincerity of their beliefs, he remained convinced that his parents had impeded his development and all but undermined his quest for truth. What is more they had left him with a sense of corrosive guilt which only a crisis in mid-life finally prompted him to address and to overcome.

It was this experience of conditionality and of the invalidation of subjective knowledge which undoubtedly served to inspire Rogers' own approach to therapy. He placed great trust in the client's experience and in his or her own essential wisdom. Rogers came to believe that the client's discovery of such inner wisdom could not take place unless he or she experienced the profound respect or unconditional positive regard of the therapist together with a sense of being deeply understood. Such respect and understanding could not be simulated by the therapist, which, in turn, placed considerable importance on the therapist's genuineness, authenticity and openness to experience. For Rogers the metaphorical white coat or professional persona were examples of bad faith and an implicit denial of the client's ability to be the expert on his or her own life. Rogers was deeply suspicious of experts and especially those who purported to be able to analyse and interpret the behaviour and inner world of another. For him the real expertise of the therapist lay in the ability to offer a relationship where a person could relax into being because he or she felt respected, understood and trusted.

When I first began my own training as a person-centred therapist I felt as if I had stumbled into a school of love. The God whom I encountered as a boy in a Bristol park and the God whom I had met again in Julian's Revelations displayed precisely the characteristics which I was now being encouraged to embody and to manifest in my work as a therapist. My life as a Christian had led me to feel profoundly loved, totally understood and in relationship to a God, who through his limitless love for me, was content to relinquish all power so that I could experience the mutuality of esteem which enlivens and affirms. I remember still the shock of recognising that in the context of a secular training for a secular role I was being equipped to exercise what were in effect god-like capacities. In short, I was being trained to love as God loves. It was much later, as I came to know Carl Rogers personally, that I experienced the bitter irony that in order to find a way of discovering and proclaiming the nature of divine love Carl had had to forsake the Church, the Christian religion and, at a conscious level, God himself. I and thousands like me, whether Christians, Buddhists, Hindus, Muslims, agnostics or atheists, owe much, possibly everything, to his courageous rejection of what stood between him and the discovery of his personal truth. When many years later he declared that what was most deeply personal was most universal, I knew what he meant.

Charlotte is desperately sad this morning. She is daring to face the pain which is the legacy of years of abuse. Her tears flow and her distress contorts her face and sends anguished shudders through her body. All I can do is to accompany her as best I can. I gently offer her tissues from time to time and attempt to indicate through my words that I am understanding at least something of her inner torment. I sense her fear and its presence strengthens my resolve not to be afraid and not to abandon her by withdrawing my attentiveness or depriving her of the fullness of my presence. I am not anxious. She may at some point invite a physical response and if she does I shall respond and not fear that she is attempting to seduce me. If she is not worthy of my trust, I am unlikely to improve the situation by underlining her untrustworthiness. Above all I try to see Charlotte as I believe God sees her. She is suffering intolerably, she is full of rage and pain, she wants sometimes not to be alive. She is also a wondrous being, beloved before time began and capable of the most amazing love herself. Julian tells me about this double vision and how to see who Charlotte really is. When this sad, hurt, self-punishing, angry and lovely young woman leaves me an hour later she gives a wan smile. I tell myself that perhaps for a moment she has had a fleeting glimpse in the mirror of my eyes of her true countenance. I am her mother and her father and her lover and perhaps, just perhaps, she might one day feel *welcomed* into the world. Is such language outrageous? Julian and other mystics speak of God's love for us in such terms. God became man, says St Athanasius, so that man might become God. Is it ridiculous for me, a person-centred therapist and a struggling Anglican Christian, to imitate God? Carl Rogers clearly did not think so but he had to turn his back on God before his experience could give him the evidence and the courage to affirm his own nature. Carl the psychologist and psychotherapist gradually found the freedom to internalise Christ, to let God invade him: he, of course, would have expressed it very differently. Julian and he, I am sure, do not now, however, experience language difficulties. I am just profoundly grateful that they enabled me to be bilingual.

Bilingualism is not by definition an unmitigated blessing. Over the years, I have had many literally bilingual clients and for some of them the ability to speak two languages has contributed in a surprising way to their sense of isolation and non-belonging. One such client referred to the 'conflict in his head', by which he meant the difficulty of knowing which language should claim his primary allegiance. To feel an equal allegiance to both languages seemed, for him, an impossible accomplishment. His sense of a firm identity seemed to demand the subordination of one to the other but the problem was that he could never decide from one day to the next which should have the pre-eminence. Another highly intelligent and sensitive woman experienced the matter differently. Her bilingualism, she claimed, made her a threat to others: she was seen as 'too clever by half' and as a result she was often shunned or attacked. A poignant example of this was the attitude of her French teacher (an Englishman) who, on discovering that she was bilingual in French and English, never wasted an opportunity to correct the smallest grammatical error in her written work but ceased himself to speak more than the odd sentence in French during the lessons she attended. In both these cases the bilingualism which should have been a source of pride and enrichment became an impediment to both an internal peace of mind and to social relationships.

Mercifully, for me, it is different. When I am worshipping in the Julian Shrine on a Friday morning, I have no difficulty in knowing that I am also a person-centred therapist who is fluent in the language of that particular tribe. Similarly as I sit with my client in the Norwich Centre I have no difficulty in acknowledging to myself that I am a liberal Catholic Anglican well versed in the theological language of that tradition. I am choosing not to use my alternative language when I am in one or other context but I am not a problem to myself in not so doing. I am, if you like, perfectly comfortable with these two configurations of myself and with the languages which they employ.

The concept of configurations of the self would not have been altogether familiar to Carl Rogers, although his view of the self as constantly in process rather than a fixed entity lends itself easily to this construct.[4] I have come to believe through experience, however, that we all have a veritable family of configurations dwelling within us and that this is utterly normal and not a sign of psychosis: to be a family of configurations is not to be suffering from multiple personality disorder or dissociative identity disorder as it is now called in the psychiatric diagnostic manuals. I am a person-centred therapist, a Catholic Anglican Christian, a Liberal Democrat, a husband, a father, a person who enjoys wine, a lover of Cyprus, a cathedral addict (hence my falling for the invitation to deliver the Sarum lectures) – and so the list could go on almost ad infinitum. Not just a family, perhaps, but a whole crowd of configurations, some of them well established and articulated, others shadowy and scarcely identifiable, some prominent in the past but now sleeping, others about to make an appearance which will be unexpected and surprising. Who, then, it might justifiably be asked, am I? I want to answer that I am all these and more and I want to offer generous hospitality to them all. I don't want some to have posh rooms on the first floor with a sea view while others are garret-dwellers or, worse, are made to live furtively in the basement because they are considered to be rather shameful characters who ought not to be in residence at all.

It is for me a joy beyond belief that as I journey with my colleagues, Carl and Julian, I can offer lavish hospitality to all the configurations which constitute my being. They will, I know, all find acceptance in the hearts of these generous companions who are not threatened by me, are not going to insist that I speak one language rather than another or that I deny some aspect of my experiencing because it does not happen to fit in with their predetermined version of reality. Julian knows what it means to trust her own experience even when that leads her into astonishing discoveries which threatened not only the doctrines promulgated by the medieval Church of her day but continue to earn the disapproval of many of her co-religionists in our own century. Carl, too, knew only too well what it meant to trust his own experience and to encourage others to do the same when his view of the person or of the nature of psycho-therapy was wildly at variance with the analytical and behavioural schools of his day and with the cognitive, solution-focused approaches so popular at the present time. With these two human beings I am free to be all of me, to celebrate my configurational complexity and even to regard with tenderness those parts of myself that I find difficult to accommodate. In short, I can enjoy intimacy with both Carl and Julian because they rejoice in my complexity and my mystery. Could it be, too, that because Carl has faith in my actualising tendency and Julian believes that there is a part of me that is joined to God and can never be separated from him, I am not afraid to relish my strength and to make friends with my vulnerability? Yes, that's it. I am not afraid to be me with all my baffling contradictions and inconsistencies. I do not need to conceal them or to be ashamed of them. Would that I could feel like that in a crowd of psychotherapists or in a Christian congregation. Perhaps – and this was a comforting thought as I delivered the Sarum Lectures – perhaps cathedral congregations are different: after all, most people in them are escaping from impossible vicars or judgemental parishioners, or just want to be anonymous. Could it be, I asked myself, that even my more bizarre configurations could find acceptance in a cathedral?

Chapter Two

A COMMUNITY OF HEALING:
GEORGE LYWARD
AND FINCHDEN MANOR

It was in 1965 that I was getting into something of a mess. At that time I was a young teacher at Eastbourne College, a minor public school on the Sussex coast, where I was employed supposedly to teach French and German. It was a stimulating place to be, not least because it was a school in transition. Under a young and dynamic headmaster,[1] the school was gradually shedding its traditional image and moving into a more democratic and liberal era. Like most boarding schools, Eastbourne College had more than its share of bruised adolescent souls struggling with the ravages of parental discord or the pain of abandonment which is often the lot of the offspring of the rich. Some of these perturbed and often turbulent adolescents found their way after teaching hours to my study door where an inadequate fledgling amateur counsellor attempted to listen and to offer well-meaning guidance and compassion.

I was in a mess because one young man who had attached himself to me was clearly experiencing emotional and mental distress well beyond the norm. Other staff were beginning to talk and it was not long before the grapevine informed me that I was developing an unhealthy relationship and should watch my step if I did not want to be accused of an illicit liaison. Although I had taken the precaution of alerting the boy's housemaster and consulting with a psychiatrist friend, I was unnerved by these veiled accusations and began seriously to doubt my own experience and judgement. I was also clear, however, that to abandon the boy would be an act of gross betrayal and would almost certainly drive him over the edge. I felt in a trap where whatever move I made was likely to lead to more difficulty and complexity. In desperation I decided to contact George Lyward.

I had never met Lyward and my knowledge of him and of his school or home or community – I did not know what to call it – was fairly minimal. What I did know, however, was that at Finchden Manor George Lyward took in former public schoolboys who had broken down or been expelled and there made it possible for them to recover and find their way in the world. It seemed to me in my mounting panic that Lyward might be able to throw some light on my predicament. What I did not know was that I was about to meet someone who would have a profound influence on my life.

To my astonishment it was Lyward himself who immediately answered my 'phone call to Finchden Manor. He listened intently to my story, made one or two sympathetic noises and then issued an invitation to visit him as soon as possible. I was both taken aback and delighted at the swiftness of this response and the very next day (it being a Saturday) set out on the rather awkward train journey to Tenterden in Kent. I have no idea now what I expected to find but nothing, I am sure, could have prepared me for the reality. Finchden Manor was what Michael Burn in his book *Mr Lyward's Answer* describes as 'a timbered black-and-white caterpillar of a house, with a long lawn and rose-garden' (Burn, 1956). The older part of the building was Jacobean and the Victorians had added an imitation extension. The building itself had an inviting appearance, a kind of warm and welcoming informality which nevertheless promised surprises. In passing, it is worth observing that Michael Burn was the only person whom Lyward had permitted to write a book about Finchden. Burn was not a psychologist or sociologist –

many of whom pestered Lyward for just such a privilege – but a journalist and poet. Lyward's condition was that Burn should join the staff of Finchden and experience the place from the inside before setting pen to paper. It is not without significance that only a poet with first-hand experiential knowledge was considered acceptable as a chronicler of life at Finchden Manor.[2]

Lyward himself answered my ring at the doorbell and ushered me in with great courtesy. His wood-panelled study (the Oak Room) seemed huge: it had a massive desk, innumerable books, a piano and many elegant *objets d'art*. If I had expected a formidable figure or a bearded wise man, I was disappointed. Lyward was in his early seventies, slightly stooped, clean shaven with twinkling eyes behind spectacles which had a tendency to slip down his nose. He had the appearance of a retired but vibrant academic who would assuredly not miss a trick. Lapsang tea was brought in on a silver tray by a pert fourteen-year-old boy who eyed me up and down with a gaze which made me feel curiously exposed and yet not altogether uncomfortable. I was later to realise that this sense of being rendered transparent and yet not adversely judged was somewhat typical of life at Finchden. Certainly there seemed to be no point whatever in being anything other than honest. Lyward later explained that almost all the young men who found their way to Finchden had spent most of their lives in a web of deceit, hypocrisy and double-talk and had collapsed or gone berserk as a result. Honesty and transparency and a preparedness not to hide behind masks or roles were not only desirable attributes but absolute necessities if a new beginning was to be possible, what Lyward described as a fresh weaning process.

He came to the point at once and it was clear that he had retained in what seemed its entirety our telephone conversation of the previous day. In his presence I felt myself both melting and gaining strength at the same time. My fears and anxieties together with my hopes and aspirations poured out of me and I experienced the kind of freedom which comes when the whole internal family is welcomed at the table of the attentive listener. I even remember breaking into French at one point, which seemed to present Lyward with no difficulty, although when he replied in Latin it was my turn to be put on my mettle. In fact, he said little but when I had exhausted my pent-up narrative he observed in an almost matter-of-fact voice that it was evident that I was my adolescent pupil's therapist and I had just better get on with it. What I suppose was remarkable was that in the presence of this unusual man I felt received and understood with all my doubts and vulnerabilities and that as a result I felt capable of discharging what was to him so self-evidently my task. My fear of the adverse judgement of my colleagues back in Eastbourne simply seemed to evaporate. I felt confirmed in my identity and now all that mattered was that I should be my pupil's therapist and be it to the best of my ability. The more shattering insight, of course, was that if I was so self-evidently my pupil's therapist might it not be that I was a therapist *tout court*. As Lyward twinkled at me over the teacups I knew that my days as a schoolmaster were numbered and that I should be returning to Finchden Manor again. In fact, over the next few years I was to go back several times and when Lyward died in 1973 it was for me a great joy that one of his last 'academic' visits had been to see me at Keele University where I was installed in my first post as a professional counsellor. It was there, too, that I discovered that the founder of Finchden Manor was himself vulnerable, a prey to doubts and at that time the helpless victim of love's unpredictabilities. His greatness lay not in his omniscience or in his omnicompetence. His strength and his vulnerability were inextricably entwined. Finchden Manor was built on suffering and woundedness transcended, not on invincibility and false expertise. I soon began to realise why Lyward could get away with quoting the Bible so readily without a trace of piety or sanctimoniousness. I could also understand why he frequently commented that all religion deserted him as soon as he entered a church building – and yet he was perhaps the most religious man I have ever met.

Lyward, when asked to define Finchden, used to call it a 'place of hospitality' although it is rumoured that he told the Queen, when asked at his investiture with the OBE in 1970, that he actually ran 'a kind of nursery'. Perhaps both definitions are appropriate. Certainly the place was characterised by a kind of old-fashioned courtesy which was slightly reminiscent of an Edwardian hotel. The courtesy, however, was not in any way a superficial veneer. It sprang from the deepest possible respect for each individual who lived, however temporarily, beneath its roof. Lyward and his staff had the ability to relate to each boy with an intuitive understanding which recognised and cherished his uniqueness. Lyward often referred to the 'tyranny of fairness', by which he meant the mistaken notion, so prevalent in schools and families, that everyone should be treated with the same scrupulous fairness out of a sense of justice. Such a response, he believed, was a denial of the individual's uniqueness and was, to some extent a pious rationale for a kind of psychological and emotional laziness which baulked at the empathic accompaniment necessary to the process of valuing the inner world of a growing boy, or of anyone else for that matter. To treat a child with the respect due to a uniquely configured human being required an investment of emotional energy which could not be short-circuited. The form of hospitality offered at Finchden Manor could vary dramatically from 'guest' to 'guest' or at different stages of the same person's period in residence. The same respect, however, was always in place even if, as was sometimes the case, a negative response had to be given to an apparently reasonable request.

I remember the events of one morning in Lyward's study which provided an astonishing example of apparent unfairness in the service of a true respect and courtesy for individual uniqueness. One boy appeared to ask if he might have another football because his had gone over the wall again and had, as I

Infinitely Beloved

remember, been punctured by a passing vehicle. To my surprise and, I must confess, discomfiture, Lyward became angry, refused the request and told the boy to clear off. Only minutes later another boy entered with the complaint that the grand piano was out of tune yet again and he was finding it impossible to do justice to the piece he was practising. Lyward calmly announced that he understood the problem and would order a new Steinway at once for the boy's private use. The remarkable thing, of course, was that both boys felt instantly known and valued by the response which they received. The first needed Lyward's anger and his 'no' so that he could be assured that he was not terrifyingly able to manipulate the world, while the second, who became an internationally renowned performer, required the affirmation of his talent and the understanding which is sadly rare in the experience of many artistic souls who are fighting for recognition and validation. Lyward's apparently outrageous unfairness was based on a deep understanding of each individual who came seeking hospitality and on his ability to trust his own response even if this took the form of anger or a determined refusal to accede to requests of apparently genuine needs.

Finchden Manor's hospitality and its tailoring to the unique requirements of each individual was also shaped by its other function as a 'kind of nursery'. Every boy who arrived at Finchden had experienced a bumpy ride through childhood and adolescence. The emotional disturbances, the delinquency, in some cases the violence and self-destructiveness, were the result of grave impediments to healthy development. Many had been the prisoners of what Lyward called 'contractual living', by which he meant the payment with conditional love for achievements determined by parents and society. The 'I will love you if . . .' syndrome was common among Finchden boys, who had often been made to feel that, as persons, they were of no value and that only their achievements could earn them passing approval. Others, again, were the products of homes where the parents' own dysfunction (often unacknowledged or denied) made it impossible for them to offer their children a reliable consistency or a predictable response. As a result the boy had spent his life trying in vain to win love and approval until the effort had proved too much and he had collapsed in despair. The stories of the lives of Finchden boys offered many variations on the same theme and in most cases it was evident that the absence of unconditional love and the non-existence of empathic accompaniment had begun at a very early stage. These were human beings who had never known what it is to see themselves mirrored in the eyes of the person who loves them and longs to understand them in all their loveliness. For most the mirror had provided a distorted image and for some there had been no mirror at all so that life had been lived in a terrifying vacuum where a sense of identity was permanently elusive. Lyward believed that in such dire circumstances (and one wonders how many millions of human beings are similarly endangered) only the most radical measures could suffice. His guests must be allowed to go back to where things had first begun to go wrong and be given the chance to grow up all over again. Finchden offered a respite (a favourite word) where the weaning process could begin afresh but this time in the company of adults and many fellow 'guests' who could offer the steady gaze in which was reflected the belovedness and the potential for becoming without which growth into humanness is all but impossible. In this way Finchden was indeed a 'kind of nursery' where the residents could often be heard comparing emotional ages and joking with each other as they wondered whether they had yet passed the nappy stage. As many were enuretic when they arrived at Finchden there was often the symbolic moment when the dry bed heralded the end of anxiety and the beginning of early childhood. Lyward sometimes referred to enuresis as 'liquidating the debt' and saw it not only as a sign of existential anxiety but also of a sense of permanent indebtedness when the nature of the debt was impossible to determine or why it had been incurred in the first place unknowable. For many Finchden boys their intrapsychic world might well have informed a Kafka novel and the level of their fear characterised his desperate and eternally guilty heroes.

The visitor to Finchden was immediately caught up in this radical plan of salvation. Lyward would never have used such language (except perhaps to himself) but the metaphor is wholly appropriate. Boys who arrived at Finchden had been all but given up for lost. They had often run the whole gamut of expulsion from school, disgrace at home, referral to child guidance clinic, juvenile court, psychiatric hospital and attempted self-destruction. Their parents, often claiming that they had 'always given him everything he asked for' were, by turns, desperate, angry, arrogant, self-pitying and, almost always, at their wits' end. Lyward, while often deeply compassionate in his response to them, was nearly always adamant that if their son was to find healing at Finchden they must refrain from interfering in his life from the moment he became a member of the community. Some of his deepest anger was reserved for those parents who, having promised to keep their distance, turned up unexpectedly or wrote letters to their offspring full of the old pressures to perform and offering rewards for rapid improvement. Some even consciously sought to undermine their son's chance of recovery by indirectly criticising or ridiculing Finchden Manor itself and Lyward's apparently permissive regime.

I say 'apparently permissive' because, in fact, Finchden's lack of structure and its commitment to the unique process of each individual had the effect of creating a space outside of time where each person had no option but to confront himself and to collaborate in his own healing. Lyward knew, however, that what he called the 'stern love' of Finchden engendered the essential intra- and interpersonal context where such responsibility could be undertaken with hope and confidence. The plan of salvation had as its cornerstone the individual's gradual realisation (and in some cases 'gradual' meant years) that he was essentially worthy of love and that he had the capacity to offer love to others. Once this realisation dawned the movement in a boy's development could be truly astonishing. Creative gifts which had previously only been glimpsed intermittently suddenly burst into full flower. Boys who for years had shunned books and intellectual endeavour developed a passionate desire for learning and would master an 'A' level in six months. Others stretched out to their parents and from the security of their own identities brought fresh hope to despairing families. Almost all of those who entered Finchden Manor found healing there and many went on to become some of the most distinguished members of their generation. When I attended the Memorial Service for Lyward at St Martin-in-the-Fields in late 1973 I was overwhelmed by the numbers present and I was also amused by the look on many a well-known face as he glimpsed another well-known face from a different generation. The look clearly posed the question: 'How on earth did you know GL?' but it was a question which already knew its answer.

In the first chapter I spoke of Julian's transformative vision of the nature and love of God and its compelling unconditionality. Her vision, so confirmatory of my own boyhood experience, sustains me as I work in the school of love which owes its origins to Carl Rogers, a man who turned his back on God to follow his own truth. In George Lyward and his astonishing 'place of hospitality' I believe I was privileged to catch a glimpse of what the Church as community might become. George Lyward, the truly religious man, was emptied of all religious feeling when he entered a church building. He, too, like Carl Rogers, had embarked on training for the Christian ministry only to opt out before ordination. It is not too fanciful, I believe, to see Finchden Manor as Lyward's attempt to create a Church he could inhabit with himself as a parish priest. Certainly it was not only a place of salvation, but also a community of healing and a source of miracles.

None of my own visits to Finchden were particularly long. When I was in the middle of my training as a person-centred counsellor I spent ten days there and that, I think, was the longest period. And yet my memory is of oceans of time. There was never a sense of pressure or of deadlines to be met. On the contrary, I recall the initial twinges of guilt at being able to stay in bed until I wanted to get up. The uncluttered nature of each day meant that encounters could occur and be prolonged if that seemed desirable. Not that such meetings were necessarily with other human beings. There always seemed to be a fine assortment of animals around to be caressed or entertained. Dogs and cats were certainly skilled social therapists at Finchden and many a boy first learned to love or to be loved with an animal. Animals are somehow less of a risk if you have been constantly criticised or rejected or had your own loving impulses scorned by human beings. There were trees, too, to be sheltered under or hugged or whispered to. Human encounters when they occurred were quite devoid of the structured, time-limited frameworks which seem to govern so much of our relating these days. I am sure there are many like me who have sometimes despaired at finding time even to be with our own partners as we struggle with an overcrowded diary. But at Finchden an encounter might take place in the corridor or in the garden or as a result of a timid knock on the door. Why it was taking place would often be unclear and its process unpredictable. Lyward believed that most of us were caught in the fond illusion that linear thinking was necessary for the accumulation of knowledge. Such an illusion was the death-knell of the imagination and of creative enquiry: 'Why start at A and go on to B' he used to ask, 'if you are really interested in K?' I remember many years later smiling with recognition when in Malcolm Bradbury's masterpiece *The History Man* students were sent to the Student Counselling Service to be cured of linear thinking (Bradbury, 1975). Lyward would wholeheartedly have approved of such a service and I can only dimly imagine what he would have made of a national curriculum with its assumption of rigid developmental stages.

Human encounters at Finchden, then, were anything but

linear. They might begin with a seemingly innocent question but it would soon be clear that the questioner was not interested in the answer. The question was merely a way of making contact, a safe approach to test out the other's preparedness to be alongside for a minute or two or, as sometimes happened, for an hour or two. Conversations triggered by these encounters could apparently roam over vast areas of seemingly unconnected ideas and events only to reveal through a chance remark a hitherto hidden facet of a boy's life. I remember the fascination of those apparently inconsequential conversations and my subsequent amazement at what they revealed and at how I, too, had relaxed into an openness of communication which was somehow symbolic of a respect for myself and for the other. That they happened at all, however, was entirely the result of the lack of pressure and the absence of a timetable. 'Take no thought for the morrow for the morrow will look after itself' might well have been one of many possible biblical mottos for Finchden and the outcome was an environment where yesterday and tomorrow were always subservient to today and whatever it might offer. It is no exaggeration to suggest that Finchden provided ideal conditions for experiencing the present moment and for discovering there a freedom from guilt and anxiety. The necessary healing began in such moments which were often at the same time experiences of deep encounter but without the heaviness or the solemnity which tend to characterise therapeutic accounts of meetings at relational depth. Finchden was home to fifty or so young men whose corporate suffering was colossal and yet it was a place of laughter, of outrageous happenings and unexpected delight. When tears flowed – as they often did – they were seen as normal, cleansing and thoroughly manly. They were as much a gift as the hilarity resulting from a boy's production of a Yorkshire pudding which had all the characteristics of a rock cake.

The failed Yorkshire pudding revealed another remarkably liberating aspect of Finchden life. Mistakes and failures were seen as just as important as so-called successes. They are, after all, great resources for learning and they provide wonderful opportunities for discovering that we are acceptable as we are and not for what we do or what we fail to do. Many boys at Finchden suffered from nagging mothers and perfectionist fathers and as a result had given up trying to do anything or defiantly pretended that they could do everything in order to avoid further humiliation. If a mistake or a failure resulted in someone else being hurt then this provided an opportunity for apologising and, if you were lucky, the experience of being forgiven. Mistakes and failures had in the past meant adverse judgement, condemnation, ridicule and the insidious shame which can rapidly lead to a sense of utter worthlessness. For many a Finchden boy the experience of getting something wrong and having this celebrated with laughter was so life-giving that it could lead to copious tears of joy. It was also powerfully releasing for staff who were let off the hook of having to get everything right and were also able, as a result, to live spontaneously in the moment. I remember one evening when Lyward called the whole House together to apologise for his own stupidity about something or other and then threw a party to mark the occasion.

Could the Church, I ask myself, capture something of the spirit of Finchden Manor? After all, most congregations are a collection of wounded souls even if the wounds are not always so obvious as those of the young men who came to Finchden as a last resort. Worship is supposed to be about giving worth to God and celebrating our own belovedness, which seems to suggest that it should enable us to enter the timelessness of eternity where anxiety and guilt fall away. Clearly our liturgical services cannot go on all day but does not the Eucharist invite us on every occasion that it is celebrated to enter the space where heaven and earth are joined and time is no more? Perhaps five minutes a week of living in that space without anxiety or guilt is more life-giving than any number of sermons let alone the tedious repetition of breast-beating confessions and the pronouncing of pompous absolutions. Laughter and freedom from nagging and perfectionism could also be the hallmarks of a vibrant Christian community, as could the readiness to apologise and to forgive. Perhaps most of all, however, Finchden's gift to the Church might lie in its ability to bring salvation and healing through the conferring of worth on every individual and in its invitation to collaboration and connectedness. Lyward never tired of showing the Finchden boys that they and everyone they met were members one of another and that the activity of loving and being loved needed every one of them. Finchden was one of the few – perhaps the only – community I have ever known where the precious uniqueness of individuals and the corporate well-being were held in awesome and healthy tension.[3] Perhaps a Church which has provided humankind with the notion of a God who is essentially relational should not find it too difficult to hold the tension between the one and the many as Finchden did in so remarkable and enduring a fashion.

Lyward's vulnerability was in many ways the source of his genius. He was an expert on woundedness and, like Julian, saw wounds not as badges of shame but as medals of honour. His own suffering and breakdown as a young man had been the road to empathic wisdom and to the assurance of a hope which lies beyond despair. It also led to his deep conviction that wounds can only truly be healed by the experience of encountering someone who was prepared to give generously and uncon-ditionally as a symbol of the giving of oneself and not as a substitute for such giving. The pathetic cries of many of the parents of boys at Finchden that they had given their son 'every-thing he asked for' revealed all too often such 'substitute giving'. Giving as Lyward understood it must always increase awareness of the giver; the gift was not the bicycle or the holiday abroad or the expensive education but the manifest willingness of the giver to extend himself or herself for love of the recipient.

It was this deep commitment to the extending of oneself in love that led to what seemed at first sight to be such unfair and haphazard behaviour on Lyward's part. There were often occasions when life at Finchden was strongly reminiscent of those New Testament parables which often cause such difficulty because they seem to commend rampant injustice. There was an occasion when a boy had gone missing and as a result had caused Lyward and the staff hours of anxiety and the involvement of police and the censorious outrage of parents. The boy was eventually located sheltering beneath a hedge some ten miles away and Lyward immediately set out in the best limousine to fetch him. The boy was welcomed back with open arms, given a gourmet meal and offered Finchden hospitality at its most lavish. It was difficult not to think of the return of the prodigal son: as far as I am aware no word of criticism was uttered and the boy never ran away again. Repeatedly Lyward's apparently unpredictable and inconsistent responses reminded me of the Lord of the vineyard who rewarded those who came at the eleventh hour with the same generosity as those who had laboured throughout the heat of the day. It was breathtakingly disturbing and it communicated a depth of understanding and a prizing of each individual which penetrated to the heart because it came from the heart.

I have concluded that Lyward was a mystic in the sense that he had, through his suffering, stumbled upon the astonishing truth that his yearning for love united him to the love inherent in the universe. Through the skilled ministrations of those who cared for him during his own breakdown, he was able to move to a deeper level of experiencing where the desire to be loved and the desire to love were encountered as two faces of the same mystery. Another way of expressing this – and here I enter an area of theological reflection of which the Western Church seems neurotically afraid – is to say that Lyward through his suffering and the response to it knew what it was to be incorporated into the life of the Holy Trinity. In short, he knew what it meant to share in the divine nature. Of course, such knowledge was probably never conceptualised in so many words and was, at best, intermittent and tentative. But it was enough to enable Lyward to trust his own nature. He knew that all that really mattered was to love and to be loved – this is the nature of divinity – and he gave himself unreservedly to being what inherently he was. This is not to suggest that he was always easy to live with for those who had no capacity to recognise who he was. On the contrary he could often appear arrogant, irrational, egotistical, even brutal. For the boys of Finchden, however, who were often on the edge of the abyss, he embodied what they, too, had it in them to become and this, not despite their woundedness and suffering, but because of them. In the same way that Jesus was instantly recognised for who he was by those who were on the verge of despair or who were outcasts of society so, too, Lyward was identified as the beacon of hope by those who had nothing more to lose and for whom pretence and deceit no longer afforded protection or a way of escape from themselves.

To see Lyward as a prototype for the priests of the postmodern age would have made him roar with laughter and yet in his most serious moments I sense that the idea would not have been altogether outrageous. He dared to be godlike because he knew what it meant to share in the eternal dance of love. And he knew this because he had accepted suffering and had been accompanied in it and through it. Woundedness was the gateway to the eternal now where guilt about the past and anxiety about the future were seen as the fruits of the sin which is known only in its outworkings. The priest who embraces the mystical pilgrimage in this way is no other-worldly contemplative. Rather does he enter the market-place as prophet and activist who is prepared to live spontaneously and courageously not because he is without self-doubt or fear but because he has glimpsed what it means to be united in mind and heart to the God from whom Julian of Norwich assures us we are never, in reality, separated.

THE SURVEILLANCE CULTURE
AND ECONOMIC IMPERIALISM

I was conducting a retreat some time ago, the theme of which was 'staying close to the heart of God'. Not surprisingly, perhaps, my addresses found much of their inspiration from the lives and writings of Mother Julian, Carl Rogers and George Lyward. Julian tells us that God is nearer to us than our own souls, and that he resides at the very heart of the holy city within us. Rogers offers a way of accepting ourselves and others which bears all the marks of the response of an infinitely compassionate God towards his beloved creation. Lyward shows us the nature of true community and in doing so exposes the processes which can lead to the destruction of persons and the dark night of despair. All three, in short, offer invaluable guidance to those who yearn to find God in the depths of their own being and to know the nature of divine intimacy.

Towards the end of the retreat a woman came to see me who had clearly been through a period of great anguish and had all but lost her sense of the presence of God. She told me that during the previous week she had been 'all but annihilated' and that the retreat had pulled her back from the very edge of the abyss of despair. Her story was not particularly dramatic but as it unfolded, I became aware that her experience revealed somewhat starkly the insidiousness of the perverse value system to which as a culture we have all but succumbed and which works powerfully against the recognition of our divine kinship. If the mark of sin is that it impedes and even derides the movement of love and so inhibits the spiritual growth of persons, then it would seem that we have indeed created a sinful culture and are reaping the inevitable rewards. Lyward's Finchden Manor offered hospitality to those who were delinquent, violent, self-denigrating, enraged, starved of validation, deprived of a sense of their own identity. Such persons, as we have seen, were often the product of wealthy homes with high-achieving parents who were unable to offer the gift of self to the growing child. It is not too fanciful, I believe, to see our current culture as increasingly programmed to bring about on a mammoth scale precisely the confusion and hopelessness which characterised so many Finchden boys when they first arrived at their last port of call.

My retreatant was a primary schoolteacher of many years' experience and clearly a highly successful one, much loved by generations of pupils. She was currently teaching a reception class of four-year-olds in a prestigious private school in a university city. Such classes are about the one remaining arena where the national curriculum, with its accompanying regime of testing and evaluating, does not yet entirely cast its pervasive shadow.[1] My retreatant – unimpeded for once by oppressive constraints – was able to be faithful to her own value system and sought to make her pupils' educational experience both enjoyable and as richly diverse as possible. She drew particularly on the natural and artistic resources of the city and its locality. She was, let us not forget, facilitating the learning of four-year-old infants and was highly conscious, as all good teachers are, that the tender souls in her care needed much loving attentiveness if they were to gain in confidence and discover or enhance a sense of self-worth. She knew she was doing a good job – that is, until the arrival of the letter.

The letter came out of the blue and was copied to the Headteacher and to the Chairman of the School Governors. Its writer was a high-powered industrialist, renowned in his field, and something of a television personality. My retreatant had met him on a number of occasions and he had always been charming to her and seemingly supportive and friendly. The letter, however, was anything but friendly. It described her as incompetent and chaotic and stated that the educational experience she was offering to her pupils was valueless. His son, he maintained, had made not an inch of academic progress during the term and as a consequence he was seriously considering asking for a refund of fees. He would, of course, be removing him from the school at the end of the term.

The effect of this hand-grenade of a letter on my retreatant had been devastating. Within minutes she had been reduced from being a confident, expressive and fun-loving person to a trembling jelly of self-doubt filled with fear for her future and overwhelming anxiety about the reaction of her Headteacher and the Chairman of the Governors. Her anxiety, furthermore, turned out to be wholly justified. The Headteacher, a personal friend who had always supported and encouraged her, was herself white with anxiety and offered only the most luke-warm noises of reassurance while stating that she did not feel that she could wholly defend her given all the circumstances. The circumstances, it turned out, included the anger of the Chairman of the Governors and the fact that the letter-writer had already stirred up trouble with other parents, who were now also concerned about the 'academic progress' of their four-year-olds. The bottom line, of course, was money. If prestigious parents started removing their children, the school would be finished. Bankruptcy and closure were just round the corner. My retreatant, in the course of a day, had become in her own eyes a failure as a teacher, a person unworthy of support and, to complete the picture, a danger to the existence of the institution which only a few hours before she had loved and served with absolute loyalty.

This sad episode merits close analysis. First and foremost, it is a spine-chilling example of the abuse of power. The complaining parent was clearly aware of his status, reputation and weighty influence. He chose to act as he did knowing full well that the recipient of his obnoxious letter would be devastated. He did not have the courtesy to speak to her about his misgivings but rather simulated a friendly disposition and then not only put the dagger in but also informed her superiors so that they, too, could join in the attack. Doubtless in his own mind his behaviour was justified because he was upholding academic standards and speaking up for his child. He had the right to demolish another human being because he held the moral high ground from which he was defending the sacred and protecting the innocent.

Let us take the analysis further. What were these 'academic standards' to which his son was apparently denied access? Could it be that this four-year-old boy was not, for example, improving his mathematical or linguistic ability? Could it be that his father attached no value to his son's developing awareness of the natural world or of his ability to relate to his peers with ease and pleasure? Could it be, in short, that the teacher's commitment to enjoyment in learning and to the nourishing of the imagination and of the sense of wonder meant nothing to him? It would seem so, for all these things were indeed happening in her classroom as she sought to lay solid foundations for the life and education of these young children who, had they been living in many European countries, would not have been in any formal school context at all for another three years. It would seem that our letter-writer was an abuser of power whose dysfunction was fired by moral indignation at a teacher's inability to implement a value system that rides roughshod over the needs of a developing infant in its obsessive dedication to the raising of so-called standards which turn out to be death-dealing rather than life-enhancing.

The insistent language of standard raising permeates not only our educational system but, progressively, every area of our national life.[2] It is a particularly cold and aggressive language. Standards, we are told, must be 'driven up', 'ratcheted up', 'forced up'. Politicians stake their reputations on their ability to play the standards game and threaten exposure and punishment on those who fail to 'meet targets'. It is a language of coercion and obsessionality, which induces fear and guilt while claiming to be a language of encouragement dedicated to creating a more equal society and to giving the public the services it deserves. It stokes the fires of competition and brings with it a whole new army of evaluators, inspectors, surveillance monitors, appraisers, quality-control experts, thought police. League tables proliferate, naming and shaming are a public sport and for the successful there is the allurement of financial reward and accelerated promotion. Standards and their 'ratcheting up' have created a culture where the workaholic neurosis is induced and admired and where half the work force seems to spend its time spying on and reporting on the other half. It is a sinister celebration of judgementalism and condemnation, which masquerades as a concern for the well-being of the nation. The fact that stress-related illnesses are at an all-time high, that the suicide rate among both young men and young women is rocketing, that children are on anti-psychotic medicine at an ever earlier age, that our divorce rate outstrips all other European countries, that our sexual behaviour as a nation grows increasingly bizarre, that alcohol abuse is endemic – none of these disturbing trends seem to alert our political masters to the possibility that the well-being of the nation, far from being enhanced, is seriously in jeopardy.

Why this obsession with standards and surveillance? The answer, it is claimed, should be immediately obvious. If as a nation we do not raise standards we are, we are told, economically doomed. Our education must be 'the best in the world', our health service – revealingly – must, according to Alan Milburn, the Secretary of State for Health, observe strict 'commercial disciplines', 'best practice' (whatever that is) must prevail in all areas of our industrial and professional life because if it does not we shall end up on the scrap-heap as a nation, unable to maintain our 'standard of living' and condemned to be in the second division in the great competition for materialistic supremacy.

We may seem to have strayed a long way from our distraught infants teacher but the line of thought and the chain of connectedness are, in fact, direct ones. A rigorously monitored national curriculum, so the argument goes, is essential if we are to have a population equipped to compete effectively in the international market-place. Schools must be constantly inspected to ensure that they are 'delivering the appropriate goods' and children must be tested almost every year so that they can be promptly assisted if they are failing to meet the government's prescribed objectives. This performance-surveillance culture is, it is claimed, necessary for the cultivation of a work-force which will ensure economic prosperity in the future. This unquestioned assumption has, as far as I know, never been empirically tested despite the fact that there are countries whose economic success does not seem to correlate at all convincingly with the mean level of educational attainment of its population. Even if it were true, however, it would scarcely be sufficient reason for the creation of a generation which shows every sign of rampant psychological disorder.

The dysfunctional educational system and the world of work are ingloriously yoked and both are permeated by the fear of failure. Here, again, reflection on the experience of the humiliated primary school teacher is instructive. She was offering her pupils an environment of learning which was free from anxiety and competitiveness. Her concern was for the development of the imagination, the fostering of relationship and the encouragement of a sense of enquiry. Her task, as she saw it, was to make it possible for her pupils to gain access to the rich resources of the world around them and to gain a deep respect for their own inner worlds and those of their contemporaries. There is absolutely nothing aggressive or competitive about these objectives: on the contrary they engender mutuality and co-operation and they ensure a connectedness with the created order. The complaining and invasive father, on the other hand, is the embodiment of manipulative power and ruthless ambition. He is determined that his son shall be effectively equipped to compete in a cut-throat world. He wants him numerate, literate and competitive so that he may cut a figure and succeed. To leave his son in the hands of a teacher who models openness to experience and encourages empathic co-operation is to risk contamination by a value system which may lead to failure in the market-place and even to a questioning of the way of being which seems increasingly obligatory in the driven world of the new capitalism.

The sociologist Richard Sennett, in his brilliant and solemn book *The Corrosion of Character*, maps this way of being with chilling acuity (Sennett, 1998). The old-fashioned virtues of loyalty, predictability, commitment and delayed gratification are no longer valued currency. Instead, the successful worker is the person who can become infinitely flexible, ready to reinvent himself or herself according to the short-term whims of a shifting economy. There is no fixed identity to cherish and cultivate but rather a willingness to be uprooted, downsized, reconstituted, made redundant, hired back in, retrained – a giddy dance of new locations and functions where only one desirable attitude remains constant. New-capitalist man or woman must know how to be independent but it is an independence that wears the mask of the smiling team member who simulates a listening attentiveness while harbouring deep distrust of colleagues, managers and company alike. In such a culture strong bonds of sharing can never develop, there can be no honourable place for service, the fear of failure is all-pervasive and the basic need for positive regard is either deemed or perceived as shameful. It is little wonder that as the technologically sophisticated advance of globalisation proceeds apace, the human race – often represented by those whose gifts of intelligence and emotional sensitivity are of the highest quality – is gradually moving towards corporate insanity. If you believe that this judgement is itself insane, then I would ask you, dear reader, to sit with me in my therapist's consulting room for a month or two. There you will meet both those who have succumbed to stress, depression and burn-out as they lose a sense of self in the frenetic attempt to perform to a tune not of their choosing and also those who, for the moment, are apparently riding on the crest of a wave, command excessive salaries and occupy positions of power and influence. Why, in any case it may be asked, do members of the second category beat their way to a therapist's door? Almost invariably the answer lies in their hazy awareness of a loneliness and a meaninglessness which they normally keep at bay by their frenzied achievement-oriented activity. Such people, who usually lack nothing that the world can offer in terms of material rewards, have become dimly aware that they no longer relate to their partners, that their children are off the rails and despise them and – perhaps worst of all – that their company or institution has little interest in them as persons but regards them rather as a clutch of competencies which today are highly valued but tomorrow may no longer be required. In short, they have begun to perceive, however intermittently, that they are disposable and, in the last analysis, alone.

In most cases, those who have collapsed and can no longer function face a long struggle before they can once more find a place in the world. They can seldom return to their former employment – even if they are wanted there – for to do so would almost certainly retrigger the anxiety and depression which brought them to their knees in the first place. If they are fortunate they may discover a new perspective and begin to value themselves and their lives differently. When they resume work such people will be concerned that this new valuing of themselves determines the nature of their activity and that they are not sacrificed on the altar of the company's mission statement or to the latest whim of a government minister obsessed with hitting targets so as to save his or her own precarious political career. Theirs will be a quite changed perception of independence. No longer will they embrace a simulated autonomy and wear the smile of the treacherously empathic and distrustful team member. Their lives will be anchored in their quest for self-acceptance and in an awareness of their need for positive regard. They will recognise, too, that independence must incorporate the ability to know when dependence is a sign of wisdom. They may even find inspiration in the self-evident truth that men and women need community if they are to flourish and that interdependence is the ultimate calling of the human race if we are truly members one of another and not merely a collection of divided and fragmented tribes and races.

In some ways I am at ease with those who have cracked beneath the strain, although I would never wish on anyone the appalling sense of failure, hopelessness and utter exhaustion which accompanies the often sudden breakdown. But such people have little left to hide. Their vulnerability is manifest and the days of posturing and image cultivation are over. Even in their depression or suicidal despair they are accessible and open to relationship. It is the successful ones who are still in post that are the cause of my darkest fears for I suspect that they are the representatives of a generation which could mark a disastrous turn in the evolution of the human species.

A few years ago, in the face of escalating freneticism in the work-place, it was jokingly asserted that nobody on his or her death-bed would express regret at not having spent more time in the office. I no longer appreciate that joke. I have a nagging suspicion that in more recent times I have met those for whom their working life has become so obsessionally important that at the hour of their death they would indeed lament the missed hours at the office or at their computer terminal. In uttering this dire judgement I have in mind a client who, having been abandoned by his wife and children, was reconciled to the inevitability of this outcome in the light of his workaholism. 'I have made my choice,' he said, 'and I can hardly blame them for making theirs.' The difference between him and an alcohol abuser was that his illness was so strongly affirmed and applauded by the organisation for which he worked that they made him a senior executive. The more addicted he became, the greater the affirmation and the greater the material rewards. Indeed, so substantial were the rewards that when the crunch came he was able to keep his wife and children in the manner to which they were accustomed while he rented a one-bedroom flat in the city centre close to his office, to which he only repaired after work at about 10 p.m. on most days. The most appalling aspect of this dismal story is that at no point did this highly intelligent man express any real regret that his wife and children had left him for lack of love. Nor did it seem to matter to him that he, in turn, had forfeited their affection. The giving and receiving of love were, it seemed, of little account compared to the compelling allurement of the work task and the conditional approval and material rewards which were heaped upon him as a result of his single-minded dedication.

There are others for whom the work environment exerts a somewhat different influence but often with equally tragic results. The office context provides in some sense a ready-made community although, as I have suggested, it is often built upon the shakiest of foundations and may prove both temporary and treacherous. Nevertheless the office provides people with whom to relate, usually on a superficial but reasonably amicable basis, and not infrequently, too, there are opportunities for furtive and usually short-lived sexual encounters. This arena is for many an apparently preferable context to that of family life with its infinitely more demanding emotional and long-term challenges. In those cases where both parties in a marriage are at work – and this is increasingly the norm in our culture – the likelihood that the work-place will become the primary context for relating becomes all the greater. Women as well as men now often speak of their work as an 'escape' from the demands of home life as if the development of a relationship in depth and the commitment to one person, let alone to the rearing of children, has become altogether too arduous. And so it is that we are witnessing a society where more and more people live on their own – many by choice – and where the birth-rate in most European countries has significantly fallen.

Those who would vigorously dispute the gravity of the situation that I am portraying are keen to point to the concept of 'quality time'. The argument goes something like this and I have heard it advanced in my own consulting room. Parents are out all day working hard to ensure a good standard of living for their family. Clearly they are not at home for their children at the end of the school day but they have ensured that alternative provision is made by the school or other agencies for the well-being of their children until they do eventually arrive home from work. Although they are exhausted, they then, so the argument runs, offer their children 'quality time'. This seems to mean being attentively present, showing an interest in their children's lives and joining in activities with them. 'I am often absent,' says a client to me, 'but when I'm there I really am present for my kids.' So successful is the 'quality time' movement that recent educational research indicates that nowadays parents spend appreciably more time with their children than was the case twenty, forty or eighty years ago. The case, it would seem, is irrefutable. Children are better cared for now than they have ever been and the emotional security of future generations is assured. It is therefore churlish of me – and flying in the face of facts – to suggest that we may be on the brink of paying a disastrous price for the shift in our social behaviour. Only a psychotherapist with his skewed view of humanity or a Christian with his absurd understanding of human nature could possibly arrive at so pessimistic an analysis.

It should first be said that I am not pessimistic. On the contrary, I am full of hope but for me that word has nothing to do with a facile optimism. Hope is a theological virtue which overrides suffering and death and moves beyond despair. I am hopeful because of and not despite the disquiet, the disturbance and the agony of spirit of which I am the privileged but appalled witness week-in and week-out in my therapist's consulting room. I sense a yearning, a frustration and sometimes a rage within the hearts and minds of many of those who seek my help. There is a deep-down knowledge and awareness that things are not as they could and should be and that human beings are failing to be what they have it within them to be. For the individual, this profound sense of unfulfilment and of 'stuckness' can become intolerable to the point of impotent desperation. 'If this is all there is, I'm not sure I want it any longer.' It is an overwhelming and engulfing feeling which can lead to self-destruction or to a cynical apathy where nothing has meaning and stoical resignation is the only response to a treadmill existence of joyless routine. If such feelings, however, lead a person to cross the therapist's threshold then hope is lurking in the wings. I am reminded of Carl Rogers' powerful image of potatoes left in a darkened attic, which nonetheless send out straggling shoots that, against all the odds, struggle towards the glimmer of light in the roof. For him, what he named the actualising tendency will fight tooth and nail to survive however unpropitious the environment. The yearning to grow is never quite extinguished and therein lies the hope waiting to be rekindled at the slightest glimpse of light in the external or internal world.

As a therapist, if the day comes when I can no longer entertain hope, then it is certain that I must withdraw from my profession. A therapist without hope no longer has faith in the potential of his or her client to grow and is therefore a dangerous companion. I suppose it is because I cannot imagine myself as a therapist without hope that it is all the more alarming that I am in my worst moments assailed by this sinister and altogether terrifying fear that as a species we may be on the brink of an evolutionary descent into the abyss. My workaholic client for whom his wife and family were the taken for granted 'collateral damage' of his pursuit of achievement, money and status seems in such moments to be the ominous straw in the wind. His neurosis, exacerbated or even caused by a perverse culture, has induced a blindness, which for the moment has the alarming characteristics of a permanent state of being. I shall now take a leap into an altogether different style of discourse. This man, it would seem, has sold his soul to the devil. He is a Faustian character of the twenty-first century but he is the product of a culture which is all set to produce such characters in their millions. That is the heart of my terror: we have created a world ruled by that old beast, Mammon, who now wears the apparel of a virtuous and intellectually agile emperor. The imperial garments include the star-spangled cloak of economic supremacy, while the imperial armamentarium has a mighty range of computerised technology and a library of manuals outlining effective strategies for achieving short-term targets, raising standards, inducing competitive motivation and re-creating identity when the terrain consists only of shifting sands. The imperial court also has its college of spin doctors whose task it is to illuminate the moral high ground and to teach the official catechism. Members of the college are men and women of impeccable virtue who truly believe that the global economy will lead to a redistribution of wealth, that the internet will put power into the hands of the people, that naming and shaming will create better opportunities for all, that flexibility and adaptability are always admirable qualities, that material affluence is what makes for the good life or, more subtly, is a necessary basis for more spiritual aspirations. The empire is indeed formidable and its tentacles are everywhere. The more it tightens its grip, the more persuasive it becomes. To resist its advance is to court marginalisation and yet as it colonises it induces a creeping blindness with potentially appalling consequences for the evolution of humankind.

The blindness, of course, is to the primacy of loving and being loved if the human spirit is to flourish and if the eventual community of humankind is to be established. Carl Rogers and George Lyward in their different ways demonstrated that broken spirits and lives can be healed if the frenzy to achieve and the fear of failure are replaced by an unconditionality of acceptance in which it becomes safe to face the wonder and mystery of being. It is such unconditionality that Julian of Norwich discovered at the heart of God and she longed for her beloved fellow Christians to share her discovery so that they too could relax into loving and being loved, secure in the knowledge that they would never be rejected. How far removed, however, is the person-centred therapist's consulting room, the serene chaos of Finchden Manor and the life of the Holy Trinity as Julian perceived it from the context of the lives of most Western men and women in our own day. Striving, competing, achieving, performing, outwitting, texting, 'phoning, e-mailing, moving, shaking, driving up standards, rooting out dead wood, downsizing, conferencing, pre-empting the market, doubling profits, appraising, evaluating, improving efficiency, fast-tracking, monitoring – the list of frenetic activities and judgemental processes is endless. And it leads to a world which is not only fast becoming the undisputed empire of Mammon but also provides a field day for sloth.

So used are we to associating this deadly sin with laziness and idleness that we forget (how apt a word) that it means forgetfulness, to which the ascetics, as the French Orthodox scholar Olivier Clément reminds us, refer as 'the greatest of all the sins'. Forgetfulness signifies the inability to be amazed, to wonder, to marvel or even to see. Sloth at its most deadly leads to blindness because it induces a kind of slumber. Those in its clutches become sleepwalkers and all too often their blindness is expressed in hyperactivity or inertia. We see, I would suggest, much evidence all around us of precisely that blindness which results from both states of being. As a therapist I am just as likely to be visited by a young executive near the point of breakdown because of his or her impressively overcrowded agenda as by a youngster out of work who has fallen prey to drugs and violence. Whatever the cause of the slothful state, the mighty sin of forgetfulness has taken hold with a vengeance. Olivier Clément describes its destructive potency with chilling insight.

> I may forget that others have as deep an inward existence as I do; I may never stop for anything; I may never be captivated by music or by a rose; I may never give thanks – since all things are rightfully mine. I may forget that all things are rooted in mystery and that mystery dwells within me. I may forget God and His creation. I may no longer know how to accept myself as a creature with an immeasurable destiny. I may forget death and the possible meaning beyond it. All this amounts to a spiritual neurosis which has to do not with sexuality – which may become the means of forgetting – but with suppressing the 'light of life' which gives meaning to others, to the smallest spec of dust as well as to myself.
>
> (Clément, 2000: 73)

The sin of sloth, of forgetfulness of who we are and whose we are, is fast becoming the collective neurosis of our contemporary culture. The fear of judgement and of failure which surveillance breeds can undermine our sense of self-worth in the twinkling of an eye as the primary school teacher with whom this chapter began so aptly and painfully demonstrated. His imperial majesty, King Mammon, can ensure that we rapidly forget that we are made for love and for loving. Into the void of utilitarianism, profitability and the correlation of price and quality come the fallen angels of envy, jealousy and hate and the neurosis intensifies. Acedia – the aversion to life, which leads to despair – comes snapping at our heels. We are done for unless we awake out of slumber and regain our sight.

When the planes struck the Twin Towers of the World Trade Center on 11 September 2001, it was precisely such an awakening which many of those in the planes and in the building experienced. Their mobile 'phones no longer crackled with the data of the commercial markets or with the estimated time of arrival home for supper. Instead they served as the channel for words of love, of thankfulness, of blessing, of eternal grace. In its grief and shock, too, the world awoke from slumber and recognised its shared inheritance and its membership of the same family. But how quickly we have fallen asleep again. What is the cost, I wonder, of keeping our eyes open and what is the nature of our calling if we believe with Julian that 'Love is his meaning' and that 'before God made us he loved us, which love has never abated and never will be'?

Chapter Four

THE REDEMPTION OF SEXUALITY
AND THE EVOLUTION
OF HUMANITY

More than a century ago Darwin electrified the world with his vision of natural history that traced man's origin through the intervening animal species to a primordial organism. Darwin's work revealed that the apparently unrelated pieces of life's mosaic actually belonged to a design of unmatched elegance and consistency. More important still, he had discovered a unifying thread in nature. The genius of Teilhard de Chardin,[1] priest and scientist, in a more recent era was to push Darwin's laws further still. He asked the question: is it not possible that the laws pertaining to life are but a special case of more general laws governing the whole universe – laws which if known would remove the apparent discontinuities between pure energy, subatomic particles, molecules, living cells, animals and man? If such general laws do indeed exist, said Teilhard, they must also incorporate consciousness, the products of thought and human society.

The cosmic vision at which Teilhard finally arrived is well known but I will restate it briefly here. I am also well aware that much of Teilhard's more speculative thought has been dismissed as theological science fiction and that there are a few theologians who see his influence as an insidious incitement to an unanchored 'new-agery'. Be that as it may, Teilhard concluded that it is in fact man's conscious life that can unlock the mystery of all that has happened in natural history. Evolution is not a random process: on the contrary once we focus attention on the progressive sharpening of awareness (on the *within* of things) instead of thinking exclusively in terms of body structure (the *without* of things) we see that at the core of matter is an irrepressible, irreversible tendency to find expression in ever clearer forms of consciousness, until it passes over the threshold of reflective thought. This threshold was for Teilhard a climactic point of supreme importance. When reflective consciousness became possible as the brain became progressively more complex, when, in short, men and women appeared, they constituted a form of life which is qualitatively different from the life forms below them on the phylogenetic scale. Men and women are not only individualised organisms, they are also persons. For Teilhard it was as if reflective consciousness as embodied in human beings was the goal towards which everything had previously been striving. In men and women the 'within' aspect of cosmic stuff reached boiling point. Is this then the end of the story? If reflective consciousness was the goal of all creation is there now nothing more to hope for? On the contrary. The arrival of humankind marked the beginning of a new stage and what is to follow can only be understood in terms of the new phenomenon of reflective consciousness and not in terms of what preceded it.

We do not need to accept the whole of Teilhard de Chardin's elaborated vision to believe that humankind is still evolving and that whether or not we steer a straight course toward our ultimate destiny will depend in no small measure upon how well we understand our own responsibilities in the task. The biblical story of creation certainly reveals a God who proceeds with great deliberation. Bit by bit he constructs his creation and at each stage he reflects on his achievement. The mind of God, as portrayed in the Book of Genesis, works methodically and with enormous care. Gradually the integrated creation appears, each part dependent upon the other – and then God creates men and women in his own image. At each stage God considers what he has done and he sees that it is good. After the creation of humankind he reflects once more and now he experiences the creation as *very* good. This is not a creator who works haphazardly: he proceeds with supreme craftsmanship and inventiveness and at every stage he pauses to confer value on what he has created. In short, he makes something and then he loves it – or perhaps we could say that because he is by nature a lover he makes something in order to love it. The loving and the making are inseparably entwined.

Here then I would suggest lies our future destiny – to be like God, infinitely creative and infinitely loving. And such is God's love and such is his desire to be loved that he has endowed us with consciousness so that we possess the ability to grasp the tiller of evolution. We can hasten the process towards our own divinisation – towards, if you will, mystical union with God – or we can retard it or even deny it completely.

The events of recent times suggest that we are living in a period where we are poised on the threshold of a momentous phase in our evolution – either we shall take a great leap forward or we shall fall into so deep an abyss that the days of Noah will be repeated on the face of the earth. I sense this knife edge within my own experience. As I consider my life today I am aware of knowing and meeting many extraordinary people and the numbers grow almost weekly. They are committed to trying to live their lives lovingly and authentically and they do all they can to resist the insidious clutches of materialism. Many of these people are also lovers of the earth – they plead for the created world to be honoured and respected and not ravaged. It could be said that they bear the marks of those who are striving to grasp the tiller of evolution. And yet, on the other hand, I am aware of a world torn apart by war, terrorism, violence and inequality, an awareness all the more acute since 11 September 2001. I see science and technology exploited and abused so that human beings are reduced to numbers and the earth is monstrously violated.

I wish at this point to affirm my own hope and belief, despite the darkness, that the current chaos, the terrorism, the conflicts between and within nations, the crumbling of institutions, even the terrifying shifts in climatic conditions are, in effect, the pains of a world in labour. Carl Rogers suggested in a book chapter written as long ago as 1980 that there is now much reason to believe that we are involved in our era in the birth pangs of a new age. I share that insight and it is the basis of my hope. Rogers, in his chapter which he entitled 'The World of Tomorrow and the Person of Tomorrow', traced the incredible upheavals which are shaking the world to a number of significant paradigm shifts which he saw as occurring at the same time (Rogers, 1980: 339–356) The notion of the paradigm shift is for me directly bound up with the operation of the Holy Spirit and with the continuity of revelation. A word of explanation is required to establish the connection between the two.

A paradigm shift occurs when a generally accepted world view, a mode of perceiving reality, receives a jolt from which it can never recover. A good example is the Copernican revolution. Once it was accepted that the earth moved round the sun, the whole structure of our culture was changed and humanity's place in the universe underwent radical reassessment. Copernicus, it will be remembered, was regarded as a heretic, as, too, was Galileo, but the fact remains that they had hit on the truth – they were, therefore, one presumes, inspired by the Holy Spirit who, we are promised, will lead us into all truth.

Why is it, I frequently ask myself, that there are so many Christians who seem to believe that God's revelation of himself ended with the resurrection of Jesus? For them the Holy Spirit does little more than send a warm glow over the faith of the prophets and apostles without seemingly breaking much new ground. And yet, when there is truth is it not legitimate to believe that the Holy Spirit is active? If we are once more in an age of paradigm shifts then does it not follow that the Holy Spirit may be at work rather energetically? Of course, it may not feel like that at all. On the contrary, it may seem that darkness is closing in and that all that is precious is being destroyed. Paradigm shifts mean radical change and when that happens the old patterns lose their meaning and bring little reassurance. Instead, men and women are left feeling unready and uncertain and the temptation is to pine for the past and to hasten to shore up the crumbling structures or to reaffirm the glories of yesteryear. Such a response betrays a lack of trust in the Spirit of God. Instead it substitutes a false reliance on the human formulation (albeit divinely inspired) of a *certain stage* in the process of God's revelation of himself rather than risking the leap of faith which comes from embracing and affirming that process itself in all its unexpectedness and mysteriousness.

The paradigm shifts which have already occurred in the last thirty years are as awe-inspiring and as far-reaching as the Copernican revolution. They concern the nature of our universe and the nature of human potentiality. They can be stated in fairly simple terms even if their implications are almost unimaginable. In the first place, our search for the basic material unit of the universe has proved fruitless. The particles of the nucleus of the atom turn out to be not solid but patterns of oscillating energy. In brief, our world, it seems, has no solidity to it. Secondly, it now looks highly likely that there is a mysterious bond of communication running through the universe which points to the interconnectedness of all events however separate they may appear to be. Theoretical physics and Eastern mysticism join hands in an understanding of the universe as a 'cosmic dance' – a dance, in the words of Carl Rogers, where every event is connected with every other event. But we do not stop there. Teilhard de Chardin's belief in an irreversible tendency in creation to find ever clearer forms of consciousness is now paralleled by the discovery of chemists and biologists that the universe is literally creating itself. It seems that the more complex a system, the greater is its potential for self-transcendence, so that we have a situation whereby the biological world is shown to have an inbuilt formative tendency, a capacity for sudden and creative change.

In the midst of all this our view of human beings is shifting rapidly as well. The work of brain scientists and experts in biofeedback shows us conclusively that mind is an entity far greater than brain and that our non-conscious intellect is capable of incredible accomplishments. Such discoveries are having the effect of making us review seriously aspects of human capacity which were recognised long ago but have remained curiously disregarded by the majority. Telepathy, precognition, healing energies, meditation are but a few which are now tested under rigorous research conditions and have, as a result, warranted scientific acceptance. We have no option but to admit that our concept of the person is undergoing bewildering and sometimes frightening change as we sense the hitherto undreamed-of potential of human beings.

Jesus, it is clear from the Gospels, operated from a perception of reality which already incorporated the paradigm shifts which I have outlined. Time and again we see him behaving with total recognition of a universe of oscillating energies so that for him it makes perfect sense to calm the violence of a storm through his own intervention or to summon fishes into the nets of the apostles after a fruitless night. Jesus, too, gives evidence of tele-pathic powers and frequently foresees the future. Most significant of all, perhaps, he constantly draws on healing energy, which, in the case of the woman with an issue of blood, seems available even without his conscious co-operation (Mark 5:25–34). It is, indeed, an illuminating exercise to consider Christ's life and ministry as the outcome of an apprehension of reality on his part which we are only now beginning to grasp thanks to the discoveries of those who are working on the very frontiers of scientific enquiry. To put it in more startling terms, we might say that Jesus was able to live and act as he did because his perception and experience of the cosmos was at least two thousand years ahead of its time. He lived, died and rose again as one already comfortably at home with the several paradigm shifts to which I have alluded.

To think of Jesus in this way is to see him as the supreme model of the new person, the prototype of the new race, which we have it within our grasp to grow towards. Jesus shows us the face of God and reminds us that our evolutionary goal is to realise our divinity. He shows us, too, what is required of us if we are to live with any hope of survival in a world where the paradigm shifts have irreversibly taken place. Science and technology have revealed to us our incredible potential for transcendence at the level of the species as well as the individual and yet it is clear that as presently constituted humankind cannot survive. If we are to prove responsible enough to collaborate in our own evolution we must learn more and more to love as God loves so that men and women can love what they create and create because they love.

The stranglehold that materialism has over most of us is perhaps the most telling single proof of the formidable obstacles that stand in the way of loving with a divine love. If we succumb to the process of entropy and deterioration instead of embracing our inner potential for self-transcendence it seems certain that our fatal attraction to material advantage will be largely to blame. Most of us are incurably materialistic and because of this we are almost infinitely manipulable. And yet if we are to begin to live in a new world where there is no solidity but only change and process, no basic material unit but only flowing energy, we need to escape from the slavery of the materialistic god. We simply cannot be Christ's messengers to science in the evolution of the new race if we are trapped in the mythology of the Gross National Product or rendered neurotic by a crisis on the stock exchange. What is more, such enslavement to materialism means that we shall never live in a world where there is some hope of the majority having sufficient food to eat.

The daily antics of politicians point to a preoccupation with materialism which is obscene, and the family, so well known to social workers, where the TV set presides over an uncarpeted council flat and children are reared on crisps and ice cream, is a mournful symbol of the insanity which is everywhere apparent. It is this same materialism which still condemns great numbers of people in our society to spend the working part of their days doing tasks unfit for the human being, that require no intelligence, call forth no creativity and are soul-destroying in their monotony. It is distressing in the extreme that Christians seem to raise as little objection as the rest of the population to this essential denial of human dignity. To do so, of course, might attract the accusation of endangering the economy of the country and suggest that there is a currency more valid than that issued by the Bank of England.

Human dignity is threatened in other ways by the reign of materialism for it is materialistic trappings that so often form the basis of aspirations and self-evaluation. Countless human lives in the Western world are blighted by the struggle for material gain or by the supposed lack of material possessions. Men and women find themselves driven compulsively by the conditioned need to acquire, while others are full of self-pity or resentment because they do not possess what they see others acquiring. All this ludicrous suffering demeans people and robs them of their potential. That is not to say that material possessions are unimportant: we need food to eat, places to live in, clothes to wear. Jesus himself never suggested otherwise and although he was on the road for the three years of his ministry we do not hear of him starving or lacking a place to sleep. He insisted, however, that we should seek first the Kingdom of God and then all these necessary things would be added unto us. Some years ago, Michael Dummett the philosopher, in a brilliant reply to the Reith lectures of Edward Norman, spoke to the point when he wrote:

> We are told that the Western nations ought, in justice, to do more to relieve and less to exploit the poverty of the Third

World countries, and that is, of course signally true; but it would probably do us some good to be told that, for our own sakes, if we want to enter the Kingdom of Heaven, we need to become poor in spirit. I take it that being poor in spirit is not an ethereal kind of poverty perfectly compatible with being rich according to the flesh, but is a matter of that attitude to material things which is content with little and ill at ease with more: but it must be admitted that that particular Beatitude is not often stressed. (Dummett, 1979)

The time has come, I feel sure, when it is precisely this Beatitude which *must* be stressed. If Christians are to live with assurance in the world of tomorrow they must affirm the unimportance of material things and show themselves fundamentally indifferent to material comforts and rewards. If money and material status symbols continue to preoccupy Christians there is no way in which such people can aid the gradual emergence of the new humanity let alone act as its embodiment. Interestingly enough, the quest for and preoccupation with materialist ends is inextricably linked to the ominous threat of terrorist attacks and chemical, biological or nuclear war. The preservation of our way of life is the avowed aim of the current war on terrorism and of all our defence strategies but such an aim is all too often embraced without insight into the materialism which characterises that way of life or into the hypocrisy which then permeates a value system that seems blind to its own contradictions.[2] The very existence of weapons of mass destruction is itself an awe-inspiring symbol of the critical point we have reached in our evolution and the fact that human beings have proved capable of creating such abominations is at one and the same time proof of the amazing creativity of our species and of its dire need for a deep awareness of the interrelatedness of all things. If we can no longer risk the folly of evaluating ourselves in terms of our possessions or of assessing our nation or culture in terms of its material well-being, even less can we dare to view the earth as a piece of property to dice with as we will. I would go even further. I believe that it is no longer justifiable to validate ourselves in terms of our philosophical or political systems. Such systems are also a form of possession – a package of ideas, principles and procedures which we would perhaps be tempted to defend even more rigorously than our land, our homes and our material possessions. My understanding of the paradigm shifts tells me that we have to turn our backs on all such impulses, however honourable they may seem and indeed may once have been.

If we are part of a creation where all is oscillating energy and where everything is connected to everything else and if, what is more, we are now on the threshold of discovering a potential within ourselves far beyond anything we have dreamed of – if all that is so, then there can never be justification for the use of weapons of mass destruction. All that matters now, I would suggest, is that as human beings we recognise that we are members one of another and that we live on a planet which must be cherished and to which we must relate with a love equal to that which we strive to show one another. The implications of all this are, of course, revolutionary. To argue, as I do, that the existence of immensely destructive weapons forces us to combat within ourselves not only our dependence on material possessions but also our dependence on philosophical, political or religious systems implies that we have already reached the point where it is *immoral* to go to war to defend our country, democracy or even Christianity itself. In short, the nuclear bomb and the computerised precision bombing technology of today, symbols of man's amazing inventiveness and of his incalculable power to destroy, demand of us a radical reappraisal of the ethics of war. Twenty years ago, the Principal of Heythrop College wrote in *The Times* words which have even greater resonance today: 'The scale of . . . destruction . . . which some calculate in grotesque terms not of individuals but of megadeaths, bursts the wineskins of old categories' (Mahoney, 1981). And yet, again, it should perhaps come as no surprise to Christians that we are required to find new ethical wineskins. We should expect the Holy Spirit to demand this of us for the whole of the earthly life of Jesus was concerned with precisely such a radical undertaking. We should not, therefore, be surprised that the unchanging nature of God continues to pose the problem of new wine. God is unchanging in his yearning for us to become more and more like him, but the implication for us is that we are to be for ever changing as we approach his eternal changelessness. How simple this is and yet how hard to grasp.

The formidable challenge to develop new categories of understanding in order to embrace the ethical stance required of us in the face of the global threat is paralleled by the work to be undertaken if we are to grapple with the new possibilities for human intimacy and personal relationships in the contemporary world. But, again, we should not be surprised. Jesus, as we see him in the Gospels, constantly flouted the relationship conventions of his day and in no sphere is this more apparent than in his response to women and in his provocative attitudes to the conventional family and to the religious leaders of his day. I am reminded of a dinner party: 'One of the Pharisees invited him to eat with him; he went to the Pharisee's house and took his place at table. A woman who was living an immoral life in the town had learned that Jesus was dining in the Pharisee's house and had brought oil of myrrh in a small flask. She took her place behind him, by his feet, weeping. His feet were wetted with her tears and she wiped them with her hair, kissing them and anointing them with the myrrh. When his host the Pharisee saw this he said to himself, "If this fellow were a real prophet, he would know who this woman is that touches him, and what sort of woman she is, a sinner." Jesus took him up and said "Simon, I have something to say to you." "Speak on, Master," said he. "Two men were in debt to a money-lender; one owed him five hundred silver pieces, the other fifty. As neither had anything to pay with he let them both off. Now, which will love him most?"

Simon replied, "I should think the one that was let off most." "You are right", said Jesus. Then turning to the woman he said to Simon, "You see this woman? I came to your house: you provided no water for my feet; but this woman has made my feet wet with her tears and wiped them with her hair. You gave me no kiss; but she has been kissing my feet ever since I came in. You did not anoint my head with oil: but she has anointed my feet with myrrh. And so, I tell you, her great love proves that her many sins have been forgiven: where little has been forgiven, little love is shown." Then he said to her, "Your sins are forgiven." ' (Luke 7:36–48, New English Bible).

Jesus' behaviour is by any standard extraordinary and warrants detailed examination. He is at a dinner party in the house of an eminent Pharisee; we can perhaps conjecture that Simon was reasonably liberal in attitude to have invited Jesus at all – unless, of course, he was motivated simply by an overwhelming curiosity. Certainly he does not seem to have been particularly courteous to his guest and has failed to observe some of the normal customs required by social politeness. The arrival of the woman from the town must have been an intense embarrassment to everyone, especially to Simon. But she is in tears and is obviously in considerable distress: to have sent her away would have seemed particularly heartless. She sits herself down as close as she can to Jesus but without interrupting the meal. Her tears fall on to Jesus' feet and it is difficult to believe that she did not intend this. She wipes his feet with her hair, kisses them repeatedly and caresses them with the oil of myrrh. Perhaps some of us know this story so well that we no longer wonder at its outrageousness. I suggest that men – especially thirty-year-old men – might fantasise what it would feel like to have their feet wept over by a prostitute and then rubbed and kissed by her continually (not just once or twice!), all this while having supper with an increasingly cen-sorious Archdeacon. But this is what Jesus not only permitted but seems to have welcomed. For him, the woman's behaviour constituted an outpouring of great love. It is difficult to imagine a more powerful eruption of the sensual, the sexual and the physical into the world of social convention and legalistic morality, and as a physical, sexual and sensual being like us, Jesus must have been deeply affected by this extraordinary episode. What is certain is that he felt deeply loved and then poured out his own love on the woman who had flouted all the conventions in order to communicate to him the passionate intensity of her devotion. (For a fuller discussion of this episode see Thorne, 1991b: 145–9.)

Today at a time when ethical and moral stances are in a state of bewildering flux, it is to my mind a tragedy that some Christians can do no better than retreat into a fundamentalist authoritarianism which would have us deny all that we have so painfully and at times courageously learned about human intimacy and sexuality in the last hundred years. There can be few periods in human history when a society so desperately needed responsible and committed people to be pioneers in the challenging world of intimacy. If Christians, nourished by the love of God who chose to reveal himself as a fully vibrant human being, cannot undertake this work, then one may ask who can. Indeed, I often feel that it is in the arena of personal relationships that the Church's mission could be most powerful and yet it is so frequently at its most cowardly and most judgemental.[3]

There are, however, some hopeful signs of a willingness to explore and to struggle with the issues of human intimacy and sexuality and these perhaps give a glimpse of an emerging Church which may one day be prepared to be gentle, subtle, non-moralistic, non-judgemental and deeply caring. Even more important, perhaps, it shows that there is an increasing number of Christians who are excited by the possibility of seeking new forms of closeness, of intimacy and of shared purpose. Guided by the Spirit and living tentatively in the world of the paradigm shifts, they dare to trust their own experience and to make their own moral judgements free of institutional constraints as they explore new forms of communication, verbal as well as non-verbal, on the level of feelings as well as of the intellect. They welcome a way of being which implies taking risks and being open to their own inner world and that of others.

It is my belief that in an age when so many people are becoming more and more divorced from their bodies and from the rest of the natural creation, and when human sexuality is more and more abused, exploited and dehumanised, the Church's task in the field of sexual ethics is particularly urgent. If we believe in the inclusiveness of the Body of Christ we may now be entering upon an era when the caring community of the Church can and should cherish and nourish a diversity of relationship patterns and life-styles within its own congregations and within society at large. A generous welcome needs to be extended to heterosexual and homosexual couples and encouragement offered to the development and maintenance of small and large communities, celibate and non-celibate, with children and without. In marriage itself there is also much scope for courageous exploration so that possessiveness can give way to mutual cherishing and liberation. But none of this will happen if we doubt the unconditional and yearning love of God and allow ourselves to be trapped instead in an ecclesiogenic neurosis which prevents us from growing in the Spirit, not because we hate sin but because we cannot endure the prospect of the morbid guilt which may afflict us if we dare to be more fully human.

Every year I go to Cyprus to celebrate the Feast of the Epiphany. For the Orthodox Church this great day is more significant than the Nativity, for the Baptism of Christ (which takes precedence in the Orthodox tradition over the visit of the Magi) proclaims to the world both the humility of Jesus who submits to the Baptism of John and also his absolute belovedness in the eyes of the Father. As I walk behind the Bishop of Paphos[4] in the surging procession to the harbour for the traditional throwing of the cross into the waters, I am reminded again of what it means to be fully human. I am with Jesus beloved to all eternity and by my baptism I, too, have the promise of the divine inheritance. The purity of heart which is the fruit of true humility and of the vanquishing of all egotistical desire is mine already if I can but claim it. My Norwich soul is enfolded in the words of Julian as she sums up the final conclusion of her years of meditation on her visions:

> And from the time that it was revealed, I desired many times to know in what was our Lord's meaning. And fifteen years after and more, I was answered in spiritual understanding, and it was said: What, do you wish to know your Lord's meaning in this thing? Know it well, love was his meaning. Who reveals it to you? Love. What did he reveal to you? Love. Why does he reveal it to you? For love. Remain in this, and you will know more of the same. But you will never know different, without end. (Colledge and Walsh, 1978: 342)

That, however, is not all. Cyprus, as even the most uninformed tourist knows, is the Island of Love and it was so before Saints Paul and Barnabas arrived on its shores and before Sergius Paulus, the sub-prefect, was converted. Not many miles from this same Paphos, where annually I now walk in the Epiphany procession, legend has it that Aphrodite[5] was born from the waves. I am a Christian pilgrim in the same place where over two thousand years ago the fervent worshippers of the Goddess of Love came to implore her blessing on their fertility, the fruitfulness of their wombs and of their crops. They came to rejoice and to give thanks for their sexuality and for their share in the creative energy of the cosmos, which the goddess from the waves embodied. As the Bishop receives back the cross from the waters, retrieved by one of the handsome young men who dive in to have the honour of rescuing and kissing the image of their Saviour, I catch a glimpse of the ancient goddess. She is not, I believe, displeased for she knows that she is witnessing her own glorification and redemption. Eros and Agape unite as the doves of peace are released and the final benediction is intoned across the waters.

LETTING GO AND LETTING BE:
THE PROCESS OF DIVINISATION

To be in the presence of someone who does not pass judgement but who extends deep understanding and total acceptance is to be able to relax into being. In such company it is possible to let go of anxiety and to be freed from the need to perform or to achieve. There comes, too, the delicious feeling which results from the experience of being loved without conditions and of internalising such love without the fear of entrapment or of subsequent indebtedness. I remember again George Lyward's amusing description of enuresis as the involuntary act of liquidising the debt. He even expressed the hope that when all was forgotten he would still be remembered for this insight. To feel indebted is to be at a disadvantage, to be at the mercy of a capricious bank manager who at any moment might call in the loan. The enuretic boy, as Lyward perceived him, lived in such fear: love for him was like an overdraft for which one ought to feel grateful even if the interest is high and the prospect of being called to account ever present. When the bed-wetting stopped, Lyward believed, the anxiety was beginning to recede and the boy had caught a glimpse of what it might mean to be loved simply because he existed and, for that reason alone, to be worthy of love.

To feel worthy of love is to be accessible to the love of the other. Sadly, however, it is precisely this accessibility which so many of us fail to provide. We do not feel worthy of love and as a result we block the movement of love when it comes towards us. As a therapist, I know only too well those excruciating moments when, full of love and compassion for my client, I experience the wall of resistance – or disbelief. The client cannot let in my love because he or she fears indebtedness or even exploitation or seduction. Love freely offered without conditions meets the frozenness of the defended heart. Warmth is refused admission because the fear is so great that it stifles the yearning. As the therapist there is nothing I can do but to go on trying to love and to wait for the fear to subside. Sometimes the waiting may last for years. I note that a moment ago I described these moments of love refused as excruciating and my language betrays the fleeting memory of the place of dereliction where God incarnate died.

I often wonder why it is in Cyprus that I feel most beloved and most open to the movement of love in the cosmos. Certainly it is the place where I also feel most erotic. Aphrodite's island exerts an influence which makes the blood course through the veins and endows me with an energy that permits an expressiveness of affection and affirmation sometimes in a most unBritish fashion. The same energy sends me each year to the museum of the Paphos Bishopric where I stand enraptured before compelling icons of the fourteenth, fifteenth and sixteenth centuries. I know the experience of being irradiated by a mysterious power which draws me to itself while at the same time guiding me into the depths of my own being. This simultaneous movement away from myself and yet into myself is the awesome effect of the icon's power. The icon painter, usually anonymous, is concerned only to draw me into the divine. As I stand, for example, before the Virgin of Infinite Tenderness with the child Jesus at her breast I am aware not only of the overwhelming compassion at the heart of the cosmos but also of the same compassion within my own heart. It is as if the more the icon enables me to let myself go into the mysteriousness of the divine energy, the more I find within myself the undeniable evidence of the same energy.

How is it, though, that it is in Cyprus that this letting go becomes so effortless, as if it is in this place that I dare most readily to risk being drawn into the heart of God? Why is it that here I find the courage to claim my divine inheritance?

I have given myself many answers to this question over the years and perhaps all of them have their particle of truth. I am, of course, on holiday: this is a holy season. The usual pressures – especially of time – are absent. There is nothing I have to do and because I am alone there are no relationships demanding my immediate attention. I am free simply to be with myself and with my own thoughts and feelings. It is a time of particular thankfulness as I reflect on my family and friends and upon my work as a therapist. I know that there are few occupations that both permit and require an entry into relational depth with all its unexpected joys and challenges. As I sip ouzo and watch the sunset over the Mediterranean, I am filled with overwhelming gratitude. There is, however, more to it than the liberation of being on holiday and the chance to reflect on the many blessings of a life lived, for the most part, in the context of relationships which offer both intimacy and intensity. Those who go on retreat know that the experience of being alone with one's thoughts and feelings is not always easy. It is often a time of confrontation with doubts, anxieties, conflicts and guilt. My solitary times in Cyprus do not spare me such experiences. If when I stand before an icon in the Byzantine Museum in Paphos, I sense my divine kinship, there are also times in the privacy of my hotel bedroom when I am conscious of my lack of courage, of inadequacy, of self-inflation and even darker parts of my wounded personality. It was in the middle of just such a time of self-questioning and self-accusation that this year, as the clouds of negativity began to pass, I stumbled on an altogether more powerful answer to my question of 'why Cyprus?'.

In 1957, as a young subaltern not yet 20 years old, I found myself in a most extraordinary situation. I was in Cyprus then, too, but this was no holiday, no time of liberation. It was the

Infinitely Beloved

period of what Greek Cypriots now call the national struggle and what, for me in 1957, was the Eoka[1] terrorist campaign. I was a young British soldier whose task it was to root out terrorism, to destroy the Eoka organisation and to reassert British authority in what was, we were told, a colony of supreme strategic importance. Within a month or so of my arrival on the island I was allotted a strange assignment. Omorphita police station was in a suburb of Nicosia and for Greek Cypriots it had already become notorious. The notoriety sprang from the fact that it had been designated as a detainee and interrogation centre. Here it was that those suspected of aiding and abetting Eoka terrorists or even of being terrorists themselves were brought for questioning. As a callow youth, it was my task to command the platoon of mostly young national servicemen from the West Country whose internal security duties in this context consisted of keeping an attentive look-out for a possible terrorist attack (a highly unlikely event) and ensuring that the detainees did not escape (an even more unlikely possibility). The police station was divided into two sections on different sides of the road. My platoon were strictly confined to one section, which, it turned out, housed only female detainees. On the other side of the road male suspects were held but their security was in the hands of military police and members of British intelligence. On no occasion throughout a three-week tour of duty was I or any of my men allowed to cross the road. The reason for this became only too apparent to me after we had been there for a few days.

The female detainees were mostly schoolgirls from the Nicosia Pancyprian Gymnasium who, it was alleged, had distributed inflammatory literature or in other ways incited unrest among the population. There were one or two older women but none more than about 35. It was a somewhat ludicrous situation: a group of young British soldiers, bored, anxious, starved of female company and an incarcerated group of young Greek Cypriot women who, in more normal times, might well have been only too happy to relate to the youthful band of Englishmen housed under the same roof. As the guard commander, I was in a bizarre buffer zone. I had the responsibility of communicating with the detainees while ensuring that my platoon members kept their distance and did not 'fraternise'. The strategy I adopted was to decree a 'buffing-up' hour each evening, during which the platoon swept and burnished the guard posts and their dormitory accommodation while I entered into conversation with the young women behind the bars of their detention rooms. Most of them spoke excellent English and I found myself looking forward to our evening conversations. I was, after all, only doing my duty, but the occasions began to feel increasingly illicit and this feeling was exacerbated by the somewhat wry comments of my platoon sergeant, a hardened but nonetheless gentle man, who suggested that the platoon scarcely needed what rapidly became an hour and a half for cleaning duties.

It surprised me that neither the seasoned sergeant nor the rest of the platoon seemed to have any interest in what was going on across the road or, if they did, they were studiously feigning ignorance. To me it was all too obvious. During the night the building opposite was often brilliantly illuminated and there was sometimes loud music. This was no party, however, for above the music it was possible to hear screams and groans and angry shouts. The bright lights prevented any kind of sleep but this was clearly intended. Sleep deprivation was but one aspect of an interrogation procedure which seemed to involve many forms of punitive and violent intimidation. It dawned on me with sickening clarity that I was the guard commander of a place where violence against individuals was being perpetrated in the service of the British government and I was supposed not to know about it. When from time to time a young lawyer named Glafcos Clerides banged on the door of the police station in order to gain access to a female client, I could tell from the grim look on his face that he was only too aware that sinister things were happening across the street in this declared war against terrorism. When not long ago I heard and approved of the many

British voices raised in protest against the American treatment of Taliban prisoners from Afghanistan, I remembered with bitter irony my days at Omorphita police station. I wondered, too, what Mr Clerides, now President of Cyprus, made of the virtuous noises.

Some nights, the terrible cries from across the road threw me into emotional turmoil. I fantasised that I would contact the left-wing press in Britain and expose the whole wretched business to the world but I knew in my heart that I was far too cowardly to do so. I rationalised that nobody would believe me anyway, that there would be a massive cover-up and that I would almost certainly be cashiered to no purpose. And so I suffered, blocked off from the guilt feelings which my cowardice, if I had fully acknowledged it, would surely have induced. I spoke to nobody about what I knew and I am sure that the platoon had no idea of my inner turbulence. Those who did know, however, intuitively and empathically, were the young women with whom I continued to enjoy my nocturnal conversations. They were the designated prisoners and I was the representative of the power they were determined to overthrow. And yet in our conversations it was I who was the prisoner – the unwilling and impotent pawn in a military and political charade which I despised. As these young women told me of their love for their motherland and of their devotion to their Church, it was I who was the one without meaning and without purpose. They were full of vitality and spirit while I was lost in ambivalence and confusion. Across the street their brothers and friends suffered for the cause and assumed the role of hero and martyr while my fellow countrymen played cards, cleaned their rifles and lamented their lack of sex. Most astonishing of all was the fact that these young women seemed to harbour no resentment towards me. On the contrary, they showed me a delicate compassion and tenderness. I did not experience pity but rather an understanding and an acceptance of my powerlessness. There was not a whisper of condemnation. When, at the end of our period at Omorphita,

I was reprimanded for leaving the sentry boxes in poor order (despite all the cleaning!) and sentenced to six extra orderly officer duties, I counted it a small price for the extraordinary cherishing which these brave schoolgirls had offered to their gaoler.

A few months later, during the summer of 1957 when Eoka had declared a truce and some semblance of normality had returned briefly to the island, I went to the races at Nicosia with the Second-in-Command of the battalion and a fellow officer. We were strolling along in civilian dress chattering aimlessly together when suddenly, as if from nowhere, two young Greek Cypriot women appeared at my side, embraced me warmly, kissed me on both cheeks and vanished as mysteriously as they had appeared into the crowd. I was hugely embarrassed and muttered some inane explanation to the Second-in-Command who, to his credit, enquired no further. Only I knew that I had received a further sign of understanding and forgiveness from those who had every reason to despise and hate me. My former detainees had been released but they still had the desire – and the courage – to let me know that they bore no grudge. On the contrary, what I experienced that afternoon was an unmerited and gratuitous love which I have never forgotten. What is more, it was offered to someone who had been an abject coward and who had colluded miserably with the perverse and brutalising behaviour of an incompetent, unimaginative and ignorant British administration.

This year in Paphos, then, the penny finally dropped. Cyprus is the place where my self-betrayal was indisputable, my dishonour exposed. My fear of ridicule, of ignominious dismissal from the army, of rejection by my peers and of total loss of esteem had prevented me – almost without a struggle – from living out my truth. And in my shame and half-conscious humiliation I was cherished by young women who conveyed to me understanding, compassion and love.

The realisation of the magnitude of this experience and its

permeating influence over the years was intensified further during my visit this year by the appearance of two remarkable books. The first, by Elenitsa Seraphim-Loizou, is the account of the 'national struggle' through the eyes of a woman who was the only female Eoka area commander. Elenitsa was the commander of Larnaca district and had under her command a band of male terrorists as well as a whole host of lesser infiltrators and agitators. Her book reveals her as an immensely courageous woman, a shrewd strategist and someone utterly committed to what she saw as the service of her country and her God. For me, however, the most startling revelation about Elenitsa was that she had been a detainee at Omorphita police station. Her book confirmed for me – as if I needed any confirmation – that all I knew and suspected about that dreadful place was true. I was made to relive, through her account, the full horror of my complicity in evil and to experience again the shame of my country and of my own moral weakness. But I learned more. I read of the extraordinary love between these young women, of their concern for one another and of their devotion to God and their Church.

> Around five o'clock we were awoken by the sound of the church bell outside Omorphita. Our heart skipped a beat. It was Christmas Day.
>
> 'Christ is born. Give Praise and rejoice. Today the world rejoices. The angels in Heaven sing Glory to God in the highest, Peace on earth and goodwill to all men.'
>
> Peace, I thought to myself. It was only a word, an impossible dream for mankind struggling in the midst of self-destruction. Perhaps one day people would mature and leave wars to one side. Instead of wasting money on arms they would use it to relieve the suffering of their fellow men. Perhaps they would understand the teachings of the Lord and make them the basis of their lives so that peace would truly reign on earth.

The sweet voices of the girls wishing me 'Happy Christmas' took my mind off these pessimistic thoughts.

'Happy Christmas girls,' I replied.

We jumped off our 'gravestones' (the stone beds), dressed, washed and knelt to pray together. Since we were obliged to go without the church services we would sing our own Christmas carols. Soon the miserable building had filled with the sweet voices of the girls. Their melody was so beautiful that you might have believed that angels were accompanying them. I have never been able to sing in tune but that morning, overwhelmed by the emotion of the moment, I quietly joined in too. (Seraphim-Loizou 2001: 180)

It is important that I state now that I am only too aware that the young women of whom I am speaking here in such glowing terms were committed to the overthrow of the British, that Eoka terrorists between 1956 and 1959 killed many British soldiers and civilians, including women, that they had in short, much blood on their hands. What is more, if a homemade bomb had exploded, they might well have killed me, too. The memory of the day when a Molotov cocktail, as it was called, was thrown at the jeep in which I was travelling but failed to go off found in Elenitsa's history of those days a strange resonance. She tells the story of hiding bomb-making equipment in a vast cargo of shoe-boxes, which served as a cover during a perilous trip from Larnaca to Nicosia. Her van was stopped no fewer than seven times at British roadblocks without, however, her incriminating equipment being discovered. Indeed, at the last roadblock a young British soldier was so impressed by the quality of the shoes that he actually purchased a pair from Elenitsa before waving her on her way (Seraphim-Loizou, 2001: 62–4).

When the bomb was thrown at my jeep, I prayed with fervent intensity that it would not explode – and my prayer was answered. When Elenitsa was stopped at the roadblocks she, too, prayed to God and the Blessed Virgin that her bomb-making equipment would not be discovered and, against all the odds, her prayer, too, was answered. She and I lived to see another day and God, it would seem, looked after both the heroine with blood on her hands and the coward who failed to stand up for truth. In her book, Elenitsa tells of her visits to the Phaneromeni Church in Nicosia in order to kiss the icons of Christ and the Blessed Virgin in thankfulness for her safe deliverance. This year I, too, went to Phaneromeni Church and kissed those same icons in thankfulness for Elenitsa and her fellow detainees who by their compassion and understanding had kept alive in me the conviction, first grasped in boyhood, that I was infinitely beloved no matter how unworthy of such love. Without such an intervention by those Greek Cypriot young women some 45 years ago, I do not know if I could have fully recognised the truth of Julian's vision, the genius of George Lyward or the mystical power of Carl Rogers' secular therapy. It was they who met me in my most shameful hour – a shame which I could not even acknowledge to myself at the time – and kept alive within me the faith that I can never be separated from God because he dwells within me and invites me to share his divinity. It was they, too, who gave me a glimpse of the flower of deep community that I was later to find in full bloom at Finchden Manor. And when two of them emerged from the crowd at Nicosia race course to embrace me they embodied the core conditions which I was later to embrace as a therapist in the tradition of Carl Rogers. If this all sounds very holy, mystical and somewhat far-fetched, let me also state, without shame, that my memory tells me that many of my young detainees were beautiful and that I was the only man – apart from their lawyers and the hated interrogators – with whom they had contact during the three weeks we were together. Eros was in the service of agape during that extraordinary time and his contribution was assuredly not insignificant.

There was a second book which contributed to my understanding of the truth that Cyprus holds in trust for me. Some years ago, I stumbled upon a German translation of a book by Kyriakos Markides, a Greek Cypriot who is now Professor of Sociology at the University of Maine in the USA. It was a book which described in fascinating detail the life and work of an astonishing lay mystic called Daskalos who was active in Cyprus until his death only a few years ago. There was something, both about the writer and about the subject, which was compelling and I subsequently followed the work of Markides with keen interest. In successive books he pursued his enquiry into the mystical world of Orthodox Christianity and revealed a vast source of spiritual knowledge and practice and showed its relevance to our disenchanted age. Inevitably his researches led him to the monasteries of Mount Athos, where two thousand monks and hermits practise the spiritual arts in order to attain oneness with God. The whole of Athonite spirituality assumes truths which Western Christianity seems to have lost sight of many centuries ago, except, that is, for its leading mystics who often found a cool reception among their co-religionists. As a result, for the Athonite monk, there is no doubt that he lives in a world infinitely larger than the visible, material reality which serves as the context for most of us most of the time. He knows that he is made so that he may live with confidence in the invisible world of the angels and the saints who are his constant companions. He recognises in his own nature, despite his many shortcomings, weaknesses and the blatant sinfulness of which he is all too painfully aware, the marks of his divine sonship. The monk's goal is to share the divinity of his Saviour, who by entering the human race opened up the gates of heaven to all believers. Divinisation or theosis is not an abstract theological concept for the Athonite monk: it is a call to a way of being appropriate for the company of the saints and for communion with God. What is more, Jesus, the Lord, is seen not as the sacrificial victim but as the prototype of the new humanity. The incarnation of God in Jesus shows the Athonite monk – and by implication shows us all – what we have it within us to become. Jesus invites us to embrace our full humanity and in so doing to claim our divinity.

For me there is an immense attractiveness and a compelling logic in Athonite spirituality. Not that I feel called to be a monk or a hermit (although I suppose the day could come). Rather do I find in this spirituality a clear expression of the truth that as a Christian and as a therapist I have known for years and am now compelled to proclaim. We are made in the image of God so that we can take our rightful place as his sons and daughters. The bitter irony is that, as a species, we refuse to accept our own natures and because of our weaknesses and wickednesses and the thoughts that they provoke (what the Athonite monks call the 'logismoi') we listen to the demonic voices that tell us we are evil and the whole of the human race with us. Some of us, however, are clearly more evil than others and must be exterminated or serve as scapegoats, as has happened since the beginning of time. Listening to the logismoi is to convince ourselves of our inner darkness and to ensure that we lose touch with the God whose essential nature we share.

In Cyprus this January, Kyriakos Markides announced in the newspapers his intention to preside over the launch of a new book. To my intense frustration, this was to take place in Paphos two days after I planned to leave the island. I was fortunate enough, however, to acquire a copy before I left thanks to the good offices of Frances at the Moufflon Bookshop, at whose side I had walked during the Epiphany procession without knowing who she was. And now the wheel comes full circle. The new book is entitled *The Mountain of Silence* and in it Markides tells the story of an astonishing revitalisation of the monastic life in Cyprus. In his earlier visit to Mount Athos, Markides had met and been captivated by a young monk called Father Maximos. It was, in fact, his intention to ask Maximos to become his key mentor in the further exploration of Christian spirituality. And then, as he is on the point of returning to Mount Athos in 1993, Markides discovers to his astonishment that Father Maximos has left the Holy Mountain and has returned to his native Cyprus. The island to which he returns is, of course, a place of tragedy and intense suffering. Since the Turkish invasion of 1974 it is a divided territory afflicted by bitter memories and with many refugees in both the Greek Cypriot and Turkish Cypriot parts. As Markides leaves with his wife on a Cyprus Airways flight from London in 1997 he reflects on the history of his homeland. From the hopeful days of 1960, when the independent Cyprus Republic was founded and Archbishop Makarios returned in triumph as its first President, there has been a bitter and long-drawn-out conflict between Christian Greek Cypriots and Muslim Turkish Cypriots, who once lived peacefully with each other but lost their mutual tolerance and respect in political wrangles and upheavals which were often not of their own making. Markides' thoughts are poignant and sad:

> . . . neither I nor Emily, sitting next to me on the four-hour Cyprus Airways flight from London to Larnaka airport on that February afternoon of 1997, were tourists, archaeologists, or pilgrims headed for Jerusalem. For us Cyprus had a different meaning; it was a homeland of intense emotions where dear friends and relatives awaited our arrival, and it was also a place of painful, traumatic memories. With all its seeming external luster of sandy beaches, sun-worshiping tourists, and all the usual trappings of high consumerism, Cyprus is a deeply troubled, divided and threatened society, a place most in need of the prayers of Athonite monks. I wondered whether those reasons had brought Father Maximos back to the island after serving as the Protos of the Holy Mountain.
>
> (Markides, 2001: 16)

Markides' meetings with Maximos reveal an astonishing work of renewal as this remarkable monk establishes or reinvigorates churches, monasteries and convents high up in the Troodos mountains and elsewhere. Young professional people – men and women – renounce their careers as doctors, engineers, nurses and lawyers in order to discover anew the magnificent spirituality of the Greek Orthodox Church. But theirs is not a flight from the world but rather a spiritual engagement with the twenty-first century. It is a search for what it means to be truly human and it draws on the treasure house of a spiritual tradition which has its origins in the earliest centuries of Christian history. It may not perhaps be irrelevant that, as I write, the prospect for the reunification of Cyprus is somewhat brighter than it has been for more than 28 years. As I remember Glafcos Clerides banging on the door of the Omorphita police station, my prayers are with him and with the ailing Turkish Cypriot leader, Rauf Denktash, as in their old age, they seek, perhaps for a final time, with the help of the United Nations, to heal the wounds to which they themselves have contributed.[2] Mother Julian assures us that from evil can come good. My own relationship with this island informs me of the same truth and for me there is a hope that lies beyond despair and which I hardly dare to articulate. As the world moves towards a terrifying precipice where race and religion fuel the flames of hatred and where Muslim, Christian, Jew and Hindu are all embroiled in appalling conflicts, could it be that Aphrodite's isle, the holy island of Paul and Barnabas, the place where Roman, Venetian, Lusignan, Ottoman and British rulers have all used and abused their power, might witness the emergence of a new stage in the history of human evolution? Could there be a letting go of prejudices, former animosities, of old concepts of both self and others, so that men and women can discover the wonder of letting themselves and others be what they have it within them to be, that is, as St Irenaeus put it a long time ago, nothing less than the glory of God exemplified and manifested in human beings fully alive?

The naïveté of this vision of a reunited Cyprus and an emerging new humanity is rendered just momentarily plausible as I dwell on the fact that Father Maximos is there and that an old lady called Elenitsa probably still kisses icons in the Phaneromeni

Church. Nor can I deny the role of the island in my own spiritual struggles. Carl Rogers and Julian of Norwich both teach me to trust my own experience, while George Lyward reassures me that strength, vulnerability, doubt, faith, anger, eroticism, intuition and lapsang tea all serve the cause of love. What they all tell me, however, as Christ told me in a Bristol park when I was nine years old, is that I am not only all right but that I have within me the necessary resources for loving and being loved in a way that can re-enchant the world: that is, if I can take the risk of accepting my own nature and not succumb to fear. But to do that I must know that when I do succumb, as I shall repeatedly, I have not ceased to possess those resources. 'Sin is behovely' says Julian 'It has to be' – but it challenges me to offer to myself the forgiveness and compassion which God for his part never ceases to make available. That perhaps is the task where we most need each other's continual help and that is why the language of judgement, condemnation and contempt can never serve the process of divinisation.

I shall end with two vignettes. The first is taken from Kyriakos Markides' book and gives a glimpse not only into the heart and mind of Father Maximos but also into the core of Orthodox spirituality.

"So what is God's justice?"

"Real justice," Father Maximos responded, raising his voice after a deep breath, "is for God to help us through His Grace to rectify that which truly wronged us. And what is that? Our estrangement from our Divine nature. Real justice means the attainment of *Theosis*, the reunification with God who created us in His own image. We are endowed with the potential of becoming God through Grace. Our ultimate goal is reunion with our Maker, our real homeland and final destination. It is exactly at the core of our being, ontologically speaking, that we have been wronged through the Fall."

"If I understand you well," I repeated, "that means justice

ultimately implies our re-entrance into Paradise, the return of the Prodigal Son to the palace."

"Precisely. When that is done, everything within ourselves will begin to work in accordance to our essential nature. Then our minds and hearts will open up and be able to perceive the things of this world with radically different lenses and criteria, spiritual criteria. At this point, justice will be experienced and function, not as commonly understood, but as total, absolute, and unconditional Divine love. Paradoxically, what we notice is that whenever humans align themselves with Divine justice as unconditional love, then the laws of logic are transcended and God works within them in such a way as to vindicate them both on earth as well as in Heaven. That's why hermits who have attained saintliness are least judgemental with people. One would expect them to be austere and intolerant of human weakness. The opposite is true."

(Markides 2001: 177)

My second vignette is of a scene which took place at the Julian Centre in Norwich and which involved a group of trainees from the University of East Anglia who were on a course of training to become person-centred therapists. But, first, a word of preliminary explanation.

About a year or so before the scene I shall shortly describe took place, a remarkable woman applied to join this course, which at that time I directed in the University. She spoke to me and my colleague for over an hour on the telephone from Kigali, the capital city of Rwanda. This was not long after the terrible period of genocide in that country when many thousands of Rwandans had been butchered by their own compatriots in bitter tribal conflict. Our caller had lost her husband, her mother and father and many other friends and relatives in the massacres. Why, I asked at the end of our conversation, did she really want to come all the way to Norwich in England to train as a person-centred therapist? Her reply to that question is etched on my memory for ever. 'I have a dim hope,' she said, 'that you might be able to restore my faith in human nature.'

Now, several months later, this extraordinary Rwandan was sitting in the middle of a community meeting of trainees at the Julian Centre on a cold winter evening. The group was wrestling, as so often, with the daunting questions and perplexities which so often confront therapists as they attempt to respond to the anguish of their clients. This woman who had suffered unimaginable grief and pain and witnessed horrific atrocities began to speak with intense passion. I do not recall the detail of what she said but the hope which emanated from her was palpable and clearly had its origin beyond the horror and despair that she had so recently experienced. She concluded, however, with unforgettable words: 'It is no use being alive,' she said. 'We must be alive, alive.' I have come to believe that in those words she presented the challenge of what it means to be fully human. To be 'alive, alive' is to risk being fully present to another in the faith that we can trust the core of our own beings. We are members one of another and are made for communion however great the divisions may appear. Our Rwandan trainee provides an inexhaustible source of inspiration. She had been plunged into the jaws of hell and found herself caught up in one of the most obscene and horrific episodes of a century characterised by violence and barbarity. When she spoke to us on the telephone from Kigali and told us that she had glimpsed in the person-centred approach to therapy the faint possibility of having her hope in humanity restored, I was awestruck. When it turned out later that her intuition had been justified and that she had indeed rediscovered hope for herself, her children and her country, I could only acknowledge that the age of miracles is not past. (See also Thorne, 2002: 85.)

Julian of Norwich, Carl Rogers, George Lyward and Father Maximos all demonstrate in their different ways what it might mean to be 'alive, alive'. They show, too, the cost of being courageous enough to run the risk of condemnation for trusting our own experience and acknowledging our divine kinship. Long ago, however, we were shown the ultimate price for such risk taking and why, nonetheless, we should not be afraid. It is the letting go of the fear which so often stands between us and our glory: 'Fear not,' the angel says, 'the intimacy for which you yearn is already yours. Behold, he whom you seek is already within you.'

A CLARION CALL TO THE CHURCH

Like all good epilogues, this will be brief. It will be clear from the preceding chapters that I believe that as a species and as a global community we face a time of unprecedented significance. We may indeed be heading for extinction. My hope is that it is still not too late for the great awakening which could herald a new dawn and point to a glorious evolution for humankind. The Church, I believe, could play a decisive role in such a transformational process but only if it reveals its most precious treasures and proclaims its deepest wisdom. For too long it has obscured the face of God through its power-mongering and guilt-inducing doctrines and practices.

What follows is a challenge to the Church to become just such a transformational agent. It takes the form of injunctions offered with love and passion. They may be considered naïve, arrogant or simply misguided. I know, however, that they come from the heart and are informed not by theoretical speculation – valuable as that can be – but by a lifetime spent with those who suffer abominably and yet have not abandoned their yearning. It has been my privilege to live in relational depth not intermittently but daily and to find God in that depth when I can bear to open my eyes and unblock my ears. I have no option but to record my findings and to spell out their implications.

To the Church, in whose arms I have been held and by whose sacraments I have been nourished since childhood, I say:

• Reveal to humankind the God whose nature is infinite love.

- Cease to speak of the God of judgement, for the justice of God is part of his infinite love and is incomprehensible to humankind.
- Lead us to the holy city within so that we may find Jesus enthroned in our own hearts.
- Proclaim to men and women that they are infinitely beloved and show them that they have the capacity to love as God loves.
- Cease any effort to occupy the moral high ground for there lies the terrain of the hypocrites and the accusers.
- Embrace and cherish both the uniqueness of persons and the mystery of our membership one of another in the Body of Christ.
- Honour the mystics and make known their passionate intensity so that praying becomes a love affair.
- Cherish those of other faiths and join with them in the search for that which gives life in abundance.
- Celebrate the gift of sexuality and let it permeate the offering of unconditional love in all its forms.
- Be at home in the invisible world so that the whole company of Heaven can accompany us in this mortal life.
- Employ the consummate creativity of which human beings are capable so that through every form of art and liturgical beauty we may find ourselves repeatedly at the very gate of Heaven.
- Become a school of love where laughter is heard and intelligence is honoured.

This is the Church for which I pray and I have glimpsed it often enough to know that it could yet save the world.

NOTES

1. Person-centred therapists work in the therapeutic tradition of the late Dr Carl Rogers (1902–87) and his associates. The approach differs significantly from both analytical and behavioural forms of therapy by placing great emphasis on the quality of the relationship between therapist and client and on the client's ability to discover within himself or herself the necessary resources for healing. In Britain this approach is strongly represented and has a flourishing national association, the British Association for the Person-Centred Approach (BAPCA).

2. At the time of writing, controversy was raging on whether or not war should be waged against Iraq as part of the American President's declared 'war on terrorism'.

1. The place of electronic communication in our culture is perhaps one of the most controversial issues of our time. It clearly has enormous power for the creation or the destruction of community. It is the basic assumption that positive outcomes will inevitably ensue which needs, however, to be questioned. The younger generation have no option but to be swept into the electronic age because their education demands their involvement at every stage. As a result, their social life is dominated by instant communication and the ceaseless incursion of 'virtual reality'.

2. The worldwide interest in the Lady Julian of Norwich and her book 'The Revelations of Divine Love' has grown enormously in the last 25 years. Not only has the book been translated into many languages but her theological insights have given rise to many scholarly and devotional studies. In the USA a new monastic community for men and women has been founded and is known as the Order of Julian of Norwich.

3. Bristol, as a major port and industrial city, was a favourite target for the German Luftwaffe in the Second World War.

4. For a detailed exploration of the existential and clinical significance of the concept of configurations, see *Person-Centred Therapy Today: New Frontiers in*

Theory and Practice, co-authored by Dave Mearns and Brian Thorne and published by Sage Publications, London, 2000.

Chapter 2: A COMMUNITY OF HEALING: GEORGE LYWARD AND FINCHDEN MANOR

1. Michael Birley, a highly successful headmaster who subsequently took the surprising step of becoming a housemaster at Marlborough College.
2. Michael Burn was also a war hero, having escaped from Colditz and engaged in other exploits to the discomforture of the German military. He is still alive, lives in North Wales and, in his nineties, has made recent television appearances as well as completing his autobiography.
3. The 'therapeutic community' movement of the 1960s was clearly influenced by Lyward's work although he received scant recognition for this. Sadly, today there are few if any such communities that continue to offer the kind of 'respite' from the freneticism of modern life which Finchden Manor provided. Instead, we have the alarming rise of 'attention deficit disorder' in the child population, which, while clearly the outcome of neglect and cultural neurosis, has been 'medicalised' and treated with the 'chemical-cosh' approach crudely represented by the drug Ritalin, the prescription of which for children rose by no less than 36 times in Britain between 1993 and 1998.

Chapter 3: THE SURVEILLANCE CULTURE AND ECONOMIC IMPERIALISM

1. Such limited freedom looks increasingly endangered. As Dr Richard House, a therapist and Steiner Waldorf early years teacher, has recently pointed out, it is not now uncommon to hear early years 'experts' routinely talking of a 'curriculum' for the under-threes! (House, R. (2002) *The Mother*, No. 4)

   Further passionate reflections not only on primary education but on the disastrous impact of the accountability culture and managerial ethics on the whole education system are contained in the recently published *Education! Education! Education!* edited by Stephen Prickett and Patricia Erskine-Hall and published by Imprint Academic (2002). This bitterly critical volume is the result of collaboration with the Higher Education Foundation, a body of university teachers most of whom have a specific Christian allegiance. A notable contributor is Archbishop Rowan Williams and a moving chapter on the growth of anxiety in the primary sector is provided by Margaret Sutcliffe, a former headmistress of a small independent school.
2. The same issue of enforced standards and targets has recently led to hospital consultants in England rejecting new NHS contracts which would have meant a 20% pay increase. The consultants' revolt has been vilified by the Health Secretary, Alan Milburn, as selfishly motivated. Revealingly, he has

---

commented : 'It's a 24/7 world in which we live and the NHS has got to become part of that world.' It does not seem to occur to the Secretary of State that it is precisely the so-called 24/7 world which is helping to fill our hospitals with unmanageable numbers of patients and to empty them of doctors and nurses.

Chapter 4: THE REDEMPTION OF SEXUALITY AND THE EVOLUTION OF HUMANITY

1. Father Pierre Teilhard de Chardin, the Jesuit geologist and palaeontologist, captured the imagination of many in the 1960s. Carl Rogers declared him as one of the 'heroes' who would finally be recognised for his greatness in the twenty-first century.
2. A strong case can be made for seeing the present catastrophic proliferation of terrorist activity as at least partially the outcome of the hypocritical political posturing of Western nations who are more interested in protecting their oil supplies and their armaments industries than in the relief of poverty, the protection of the planet and the emergence of a more just world.
3. A recent lamentable example of such cowardice and judgementalism has been the opposition to the appointment of Dr Rowan Williams as Archbishop of Canterbury by strident evangelical minority groups in the Church of England. The added irony is that Dr Williams, a towering figure in international theological circles, is accused of not knowing his Bible!
4. Paphos was the seat of Sergius Paulus, the Roman sub-prefect who was converted by the preaching of St Paul and St Barnabas. It has been a bishopric of the Antocephalous Greek Orthodox Church of Cyprus since earliest times and has survived earthquakes, invasions and persecutions. Until recently no more than a small fishing town, it has since the Turkish invasion of Cyprus in 1974 become a home to many Greek Cypriot refugees and is now a flourishing tourist resort. The present bishop is His Eminence Metropolitan Chrysostomos, whose enthusiastic support, together with that of the other Cyprus Bishops, made it possible for the A G Leventis Foundation to sponsor an exhibition of Cypriot icons at the Hellenic Centre in London during November and December 2000.
5. Aphrodite, the goddess of love, was reputedly born but a mile or two from one of the remaining British 'sovereign bases' on the island.

Chapter 5: LETTING GO AND LETTING BE: THE PROCESS OF DIVINISATION

1. Eoka was the Greek acronym for the National Organisation of Cypriot Fighters. It began operations on 1 April 1955 and remained a potent force on the island until Cyprus became an independent republic in 1960. Its

military leader, known as Dighenis, the name of a Byzantine hero, was Colonel (later General) George Grivas. Archbishop Makarios III, the first President of Cyprus, undoubtedly provided the political inspiration for Eoka, in his role as Ethnarch and leader of the Greek Cypriot people during the final years of British rule.

2. From January 2002, Clerides and Denktash met weekly well into the summer in an attempt to find a solution to the island's bitter division. Denktash became seriously ill in October but further impetus for some form of reunification was given by the announcement of the Republic of Cyprus's forthcoming admission to the European Union in 2004. With startling celerity this was followed by the election of a new government in Turkey and the presentation of a United Nations draft solution of the Cyprus problem. A recovering Denktash and a determined Clerides resumed their negotiations as hope grew of an agreed settlement. Whatever the ultimate outcome might be, it became increasingly clear that only a spiritual evolution of immense dimensions could guarantee a lasting peace. Sadly, by March 2003, despite intensive efforts by United Nations Secretary-General Kofi Annan, a settlement had still not been achieved. Amazingly, hope was rekindled on 23 April when the Turkish Cypriot side threw open the heavily guarded border for the first time in 29 years.

LIST OF REFERENCES

Bradbury, M. (1975) *The History Man*, London, Secker & Warburg.

Burn, M. (1956) *Mr Lyward's Answer*, London, Hamish Hamilton.

Clément, O. (2000) *Three Prayers* (tr. Michael Breck), New York, St Vladimir's Seminary Press.

Colledge, E. and Walsh J. (eds) (1978) *Julian of Norwich: Showings*, New York, Paulist Press.

Dummett, M. (1979) *A response to the Reith Lectures of Dr Edward Norman*, London, Occasional Publication, Catholic Institute for International Relations.

Mahoney, J. (1981) 'The difficulties of defining a "just war" in the nuclear age', *The Times*, 21 February.

Markides, K. (2001) *The Mountain of Silence*, New York, Doubleday.

Mearns, D. and Thorne, B. (1999) *Person-Centred Counselling in Action*, second edition, London, Sage Publications.

Rogers, C.R. (1980) *A Way of Being*, Boston, Houghton Mifflin.

Sennett, R. (1998) *The Corrosion of Character*, New York, W.W. Norton & Co.

Seraphim-Loizou, E. (2001) *The Cyprus Liberation Struggle 1955–1959*, (tr. John Vickers), Nicosia, Epiphaniou Publications.

Thorne, B. (1985) *The Quality of Tenderness*, Norwich, Norwich Centre Publications.

Thorne, B. (1991a) *Behold the Man*, London, Darton, Longman and Todd.

Thorne, B. (1991b) *Person-Centred Counselling: Therapeutic and Spiritual Dimensions*, London, Whurr Publishers.

Thorne, B. (1992) *Carl Rogers*, London, Sage Publications.

Thorne, B. (2002) *The Mystical Power of Person-Centred Therapy*, London, Whurr Publishers.

Vitz, P. (1977) *Psychology as Religion: the Cult of Self-Worship*, Grand Rapids MI, William B. Eerdmans.